MW01608482

Tagine Greats: 80 Delicious Tagine Recipes, the Top 80 Moroccan Tajine recipes

Copyright © 2009

Notice of rights

All rights reserved. No part of this book may be reproduced or transmitted in any form by any means, electronic, mechanical, photocopying, recording, or otherwise, without the prior written permission of the publisher.

Notice of Liability

The information in this book is distributed on an "As Is" basis without warranty. While every precaution has been taken in the preparation of the book, neither the author nor the publisher shall have any liability to any person or entity with respect to any loss or damage caused or alleged to be caused directly or indirectly by the instructions contained in this book or by the products described in it.

Trademarks

Many of the designations used by manufacturers and sellers to distinguish their products are claimed as trademarks. Where those designations appear in this book, and the publisher was aware of a trademark claim, the designations appear as requested by the owner of the trademark. All other product names and services identified throughout this book are used in editorial fashion only and for the benefit of such companies with no intention of infringement of the trademark. No such use, or the use of any trade name, is intended to convey endorsement or other affiliation with this book.

Welcome

If you own a tagine, you need this book. If you don't own one, you are missing out. They are a great way to cook and the food is simply beautiful. If you love Moroccan food then this recipe book is a must have.

You'll love this book, the recipes are easy, the ingredients are easy to get and they don't take long to make.

There is an excellent recipe for Tagine of Okra and Tomatoes and a wonderful Vegetable Tagine with Sliced Apricots at the back of the book. My favorite tagines are the slightly sweet ones with dates, prunes, apricots and the different types of nuts that are added toward the end of the cooking time. There is also a wonderful Lamb Tagine With Apricots, Olives and Buttered Almonds. There is also a really nice minced beef tagine with wonderfully tasting preserved lemons which are very easy to make yourself.

This book will also give you enough inspiration to experiment with different ingredients since you'll find the extensive index to be extremely helpful.

The recipes are superb. Wonderfully easy to put together and you don't have to make or purchase a ton of condiments before you have a chance to play with them.

Yummy!! Definitely great comfort food during winter. And don't forget the couscous!

Table Of Contents

Contents

Tagine Background

A tajine or tagine (pronounced /t□□□□i□n/; Arabic: طاج ني , IPA: [t□a□d□i□n]) is a type of dish found in the North African cuisines of Morocco, which is named after the special pot in which it is cooked. The traditional tajine pot is formed entirely of a heavy clay which is sometimes painted or glazed. It consists of two parts; a base unit which is flat and circular with low sides, and a large cone or dome-shaped cover that rests inside the base during cooking. The cover is so designed to promote the return of all condensation to the bottom. With the cover removed, the base can be taken to the table for serving.

Recently, European manufacturers have created tajines with heavy cast iron bottoms that can be fired on a stovetop at high heat. This permits browning meat and vegetables before cooking. While the similar Dutch oven and Sač spell (sach) (a cast iron pot with a tight cover) braises most efficiently in the oven, the tajine braises best on the stovetop.

Moroccan Tajine

Tajines in Moroccan cuisine are slow-cooked stews braised at low temperatures, resulting in tender meat with aromatic vegetables and sauce. They are traditionally cooked in the tajine pot, whose cover has a knob-like handle at its top to facilitate removal. While simmering, the cover can be lifted off without the aid of a mitten, enabling the cook to inspect the main ingredients, add vegetables, move things around, or add additional braising liquid. Most tajines involve slow simmering of less-expensive meats. For example, the ideal cuts of lamb are the neck, shoulder or shank cooked until it is falling off the bone. Very few Moroccan tajines require initial browning; if there is to be browning it is invariably done after the lamb has been simmered and the flesh has become butter-tender and very moist. In order to accomplish this, the cooking liquid must contain some fat, which may be skimmed off later.

Moroccan tajines often combine lamb or chicken with a medley of ingredients or seasonings: olives, quinces, apples, pears, apricots, raisins, prunes, dates, nuts, with fresh or preserved lemons, with or without honey, with or without a complexity of spices. Traditional spices that are used to flavour tajines include ground cinnamon, saffron, ginger, turmeric, cumin, paprika, pepper, as well as the famous spice blend Ras el hanout. Some famous tajine dishes are mqualli or mshermel (both are pairings of chicken, olives and citrus fruits, though preparation methods differ), kefta (meatballs in an egg and tomato sauce), and mrouzia (lamb, raisins and almonds). Other ingredients for a tajine may include any product that braises well: fish, quail, pigeon, beef, root vegetables, legumes, even amber and agarwood. Modern recipes in the West include pot roasts, ossobuco, lamb shanks and turkey legs. Seasonings can be traditional Moroccan spices, French, Italian or suited to the dish.

Tunisian tajine

What Tunisians refer to as a "tajine" is very different from the more well-known Moroccan dish.

Tunisian tajine is more like an Italian frittata. First, a simple ragout of meat cut into very small pieces, cooked with onions and various spices, such as a blend of dried rosebuds and ground cinnamon known as bharat, or a robust combination of ground coriander and caraway seeds, is called tabil.

Then something starchy is added to thicken the juices - common thickeners include cannellini beans, chickpeas, breadcrumbs or cubed potatoes. When the meat is tender, it is combined with whatever ingredient has been chosen to be the dominant flavoring. Examples include but are not limited to fresh parsley, dried mint, saffron, sundried tomatoes, cooked vegetables, or even stewed calf's brains. Next, the stew is enriched with cheese and eggs. Finally, this egg & stew is baked in a deep pie dish, either on the stove or in the oven until both top and bottom are crisply cooked and the eggs are just set.

When the tajine is ready, it is turned out onto a plate and sliced into squares, accompanied by wedges of lemon. Tunisian tajines can be made with seafood, or as a completely vegetarian dish. In rural parts of Tunisia, home cooks place a shallow earthenware dish over glowing olive wood, fill it, cover it with a flat earthen pan, and then pile hot coals on top. The resulting tajine is crusty on top and bottom, moist within, and is infused with a subtle smoky fragrance.

Now on the recipes!

This article is licensed under the GNU Free Documentation License. It uses material from the Wikipedia article "Tagine".Source http://en.wikipedia.org/wiki/Tagine

African Mixed Vegetable Tajine

This chunky vegetable North African stew is great served with rice or couscous.It sounds weird, but raisins are common in stews like these. If you're skeptical, eliminate them. You'll still have a wonderful stew.

1 cup	dry chickpeas (garbanzo beans)	
2 Tbs	olive oil	
2 cups	chopped onion	
2	cloves garlic, minced	
1 cup	sliced carrots	
2	fresh green chilies, like jalapenos, seeds and stems removed, sliced	
1 cup	sliced zucchini	
2 cups	chopped tomatoes	

1	tsp	ground cumin
1	tsp	salt
1/4	tsp	(freshly ground) black pepper
2 1/2	cups	vegetable stock or chicken stock
1/2	cup	raisins
		Juice of 1 lemon
1/4	cup	chopped green onions, white part only
2	Tbs	chopped fresh cilantro

Procedure

1 Drain and rinse the chickpeas. Put them in a large, heavy casserole covered with cold water. Bring to a boil and cook chickpeas until tender, about 1 hour. The cooking time depends on the age of the chickpeas. Drain chickpeas, chop them coarsely and set aside.

2 Heat the oil in a large, heavy skillet and sauté the onion, garlic, carrots, chilies and zucchini for 3 minutes. Add the tomatoes, cumin, salt and pepper and simmer for 2 minutes.

3 Add the stock and raisins, and bring the mixture to a boil. Add the chopped chickpeas to the boiling mixture, reduce the heat to a simmer, cover and simmer for 25 minutes.

4 Stir in the lemon juice, scallions and cilantro, and serve.

Servings: 6

Beef Tajine with Prunes

3	lbs	beef -- cubed 1" alcatra	1/2 lb	pitted prunes
3		onions -- chopped	3 Tbs	sesame seeds
1	Tbs	grated ginger	2 Tbs	oil
1		small garlic clove -- minced	1 Tbs	butter.
1	tsp	saffron		salt and pepper
1	tsp	cumin		

Procedure

1 Heat oil. Add butter. When butter starts to foam add beef to pan.Cook until all liquid has evaporated. Stir in onions,garlic,ginger,saffron,cumin,salt and pepper.Cook until almost dry.

2 Add 1/2 cup water, cover pan, turn down heat and simmer for 2 hours adding more water as needed.

3 When beef is tender add prunes and cook 10 mins more.

4 Check seasonings. Serve hot sprinkled with sesame seeds.

5 I serve it with couscous mixed with chickpeas.

Servings: 4

Cauliflower Tagine

3/4 cup extra-virgin olive oil
1 large onion, thinly sliced
10 garlic cloves, finely chopped
1 green bell pepper, thinly sliced
2 Tbs sweet paprika
2 Tbs Tabil
1 Tbs tomato paste
Salt and freshly ground pepper

1/4 cup thinly sliced oil-packed sun-dried tomatoes, drained
1/2 cup water
One 2 1/2 -pound cauliflower, cored and cut into 2-inch florets
1 cup fine dry bread crumbs
3 oz Gruyère cheese, shredded (1 cup)
5 large eggs, beaten

Procedure

1 Preheat the oven to 400°. Lightly grease a 9-by-13-inch glass or ceramic baking dish. In a large skillet, heat the olive oil. Add the onion and cook over low heat, stirring occasionally, until softened, about 8 minutes. Add the garlic, bell pepper, paprika, Tabil, tomato paste and a pinch each of salt and pepper. Cover and cook, stirring occasionally, until the pepper softens, about 7 minutes. Add the sun-dried tomatoes and water and simmer for 1 minute. Season with salt and pepper and transfer to the prepared baking dish.

2 In a large pot of boiling salted water, cook the cauliflower until just tender, about 5 minutes. Drain and pat dry. Spread the cauliflower in the baking dish.

3 In a small bowl, toss the bread crumbs with the Gruyère and season with salt and pepper. Stir in the beaten eggs and pour the mixture over the cauliflower. Cover with foil and bake in the upper third of the oven for 15 minutes, or until bubbling around the edges. Uncover and bake for about 15 minutes longer, until browned and crisp on top. Let the tagine stand for 10 minutes before serving.

Servings: 6

Author Notes

The recipe can be prepared ahead through Step 2 and refrigerated separately. Bring to room temperature before proceeding.

Chicken Tagine

An amazing Moroccan cook named Naima taught me to make this dish. If you ever have the chance to buy a tagine (a clay cooking pot) it is worth it just to make this dish. Serve the finished meal boiling hot and eat it the traditional way -- straight from the clay tagine. By the way, I have adjusted this recipe to use chicken breasts (which are more common in the West) but in Morocco you would more likely get a cut such as a thigh. Any piece of chicken will work just fine.

* 3-4 chicken breasts
* 2 cloves garlic, chopped
* 1-2 small onions, sliced into rings
* 1 teaspoon turmeric
* 1/4 cup oil (not olive oil)

* salt and pepper
* 3-4 carrots, peeled and quartered lengthwise
* 1-2 potatoes, cut into bite sized pieces
* 1-2 tomatoes, cut into wedges
* olive, to garnish

Procedure

1 Heat the oil in the tagine over a low heat and sauté the garlic and onions for a couple minutes.
2 Mix in some turmeric, then lay the chicken breasts on the bottom and season with salt and pepper.
3 Cover and let the chicken brown on one side, turn and continue cooking until the other side is brown.
4 Spread the carrots and potatoes evenly around the meat, add about 1/2 cup water and then cover again.
5 Continue cooking over a low heat.
6 When the vegetables are nearly cooked, sprinkle the tomato wedges over the top along with some more salt and pepper.
7 Cover and cook until the vegetables are done.
8 Add a few olives, if desired.
9 Bring to the table while it is still bubbling.

Servings: 3

Preparation Time: 10 minutes

Cooking Time: 40 minutes

Chicken Tagine

3	Tbs	olive oil
1 1/2	lbs	skinless boneless chicken breast, cut into strips, and patted dry
1 1/2	cups	sliced onions
1 1/2	cups	coarsely-chopped green bell pepper, (abt 1" pieces)
1 1/2	cups	thickly-sliced carrots
1 1/2	cups	thickly-sliced celery
3		garlic cloves, peeled, left whole
		Salt, to taste
		Freshly-ground black pepper, to taste
2	tsp	ground cumin
1/2	tsp	ground coriander
3		bay leaves
2	cups	cubed (1") firm ripe plum or other tomatoes
2	cups	cauliflower florets
6	cups	water
1		chicken bouillon cube
1		lemon - (or to taste), cut into slices
2	cups	couscous
1/8	tsp	Harissa paste - (to 1/4)

Procedure

1 In a casserole set over moderately-high heat, warm 1 tablespoon of the oil until hot. Add the chicken and cook, stirring, until no longer pink. With a slotted spoon transfer to a plate.

2 Add the remaining oil to the casserole, the onions, pepper, carrots, celery, garlic, salt, pepper, cumin, coriander, and bay leaves, and cook the mixture over moderate heat, covered, stirring occasionally, for 5 minutes.

3 Add the tomatoes and cauliflower and cook, stirring, 3 minutes more. Add the water, bouillon cube, and lemon slices, bring to a boil, and simmer, covered, 5 minutes, or until vegetables are just tender.

4 Return the chicken to the casserole, add the couscous, and cook over moderate heat, stirring, for 2 minutes. Add the Harissa paste and salt to taste, stir to combine and let stand,

7

covered, off the heat 5 minutes. Remove and discard bay leaves before serving.

Servings: 6

Chicken Tagine

1/2		chicken, cut up
1		medium onion chopped
2		cloves garlic minced
1	Tbs	olive oil
1	lb	fresh (or canned)Roma tomatoes chopped.
1/2 tsp		salt
1		dried lime (or juice of fresh lime)

1 tsp ground toasted cumin seeds
1 tsp ground toasted coriander seeds
1 tsp ground cinnamon
1 tsp turmeric
1 tsp black pepper
1 teapoon crushed red chili peppers
1 tsp grated ginger root

Procedure

1 In a heavy pan (dutch oven) brown chicken pieces in oil over medium-high heat.
2 Remove chicken pieces, and drain excess fat, leaving about one Tablespoon.
3 Saute onions until translucent. Add garlic, and contiue frying for another minute.
4 Add ginger, and remaining spices, and fry for another minute.
5 Return chicken pieces to pot, and add tomatoes, limes, and salt.
6 Simmer, covered, for about 30 minutes.
7 Serve on a bed of rice.

Servings: 4

Author Notes

This is a basic recipe. Recipe can be varied by adding,toward the end, one cup of one of the following okra, cooked white beans, potatoes, green beans, etc...

Chicken Tagine

1	Tbs	olive oil,
6		boneless, skinless chicken breast halves, salt, pepper,
1		onion chopped,
2		cloves garlic-chopped,
1/2 tsp		ground cummin,

1/2 tsp	ground coriander,
2	medium tomatoes, seeded and chopped (about 1-1/2 cups)
1/2 tsp	red pepper flakes,
1/2 cup	chicken broth, green chiles(green pepper), cut into thin strips, for garnish.

Procedure

1 Heat oil in a large nonstick pan over medium heat. Season chicken with salt and pepper. Place chicken in pan and cook until brown, about 6 minutes per side. Remove chicken and set aside. Add onion and garlic to pan.

2 Cook on medium heat until light browned, about 3 min. Add cumin and coriander and cook for another minute.

3 Add tomatoes, chicken broth and red peppers. Bring to boil. return chicken to pan with any juices.

4 Cover and let it simmer for 20 min. or until cooked. Serve and Enjoy.

5 Add green chiles in thin strips for garnish.

Servings: 4

Chicken Tagine

"This Moroccan slow cooker dish is the perfect blend of sweetness and spice."

* 30 ml olive oil
* 8 skinless, boneless chicken thighs, cut into 1-inch pieces
* 1 eggplant, cut into 1 inch cubes
* 2 large onions, thinly sliced
* 4 large carrots, thinly sliced
* 60 g dried cranberries
* 65 g chopped dried apricots
* 475 ml chicken broth
* 30 g tomato paste

* 30 ml lemon juice
* 15 g all-purpose flour
* 10 g garlic salt
* 3 g ground cumin
* 3 g ground ginger
* 2 g cinnamon
* 2 g ground black pepper
* 235 ml water
* 175 g couscous

Procedure

1 Heat olive oil in a skillet over medium-high heat. Place the chicken pieces and eggplant in the heated oil; stir and cook until the chicken is browned on all sides but not cooked through. Remove the skillet from the heat.

2 Place the browned chicken and eggplant on the bottom of a slow cooker. Layer the onion, carrots, dried cranberries, and apricots over the chicken.

3 Whisk together the chicken broth, tomato paste, lemon juice, flour, garlic salt, cumin, ginger, cinnamon, and ground black pepper in a bowl. Pour the broth mixture into the slow cooker with the chicken and vegetables.

4 Cook on High setting for 5 hours, or on Low setting for 8 hours.

5 Bring water to boil in a saucepan. Stir in couscous, and remove from heat. Cover, and let stand about 5 minutes, until liquid has been absorbed. Fluff with a fork.

Servings: 8

Preparation Time: 30 minutes
Cooking Time: 300 minutes
Total Time: 330 minutes

Chicken Tagine with Apricots and Almonds

* 1 teaspoon ground cinnamon
* 1 teaspoon ground ginger
* 1/2 teaspoon turmeric
* 1/2 teaspoon black pepper
* 1 1/4 teaspoons salt
* 3 tablespoons plus 1/4 cup olive oil
* 1 (3-lb) chicken, cut into 6 pieces, wings and backbone discarded
* 1 tablespoon unsalted butter
* 1 medium red onion, halved, then sliced 1/4 inch thick
* 4 garlic cloves, finely chopped
* 5 fresh cilantro
* 5 sprigs fresh flat-leaf parsley
* 1 1/2 cups water
* 2 tablespoons mild honey
* 1 (3-inch) cinnamon stick
* 1/2 cup dried Turkish apricots, separated into halves
* 1/3 cup whole blanched almonds
* Special equipment: a 10- to 12-inch tagine or heavy skillet; kitchen string

Procedure

1 Stir together ground cinnamon, ginger, turmeric, pepper, 1 teaspoon salt, and 2 tablespoons oil in a large bowl. Add chicken and turn to coat well.

2 Heat butter and 1 tablespoon oil in base of tagine (or in skillet), uncovered, over moderate heat until hot but not smoking, then brown half of chicken, skin sides down, turning over once, 8 to 12 minutes. Transfer to a plate. Brown remaining chicken in same manner, adding any spice mixture left in bowl.

3 Add onion and remaining 1/4 teaspoon salt to tagine and cook, uncovered, stirring frequently, until soft, about 8 minutes. Add garlic and cook, stirring occasionally, 3 minutes. Tie cilantro and parsley into a bundle with kitchen string and add to tagine along with 1/2 cup water, chicken,

13

and any juices accumulated on plate. Reduce heat and simmer, covered, 30 minutes.

4 While chicken cooks, bring honey, remaining cup water, cinnamon stick, and apricots to a boil in a 1- to 2-quart heavy saucepan, then reduce heat and simmer, uncovered, until apricots are very tender (add more water if necessary). Once apricots are tender, simmer until liquid is reduced to a glaze, 10 to 15 minutes.

5 While apricots cook, heat remaining 1/4 cup oil in a small skillet over moderate heat and cook almonds, stirring occasionally, until just golden, 1 to 2 minutes. Transfer with a slotted spoon to paper towels to drain.

6 Ten minutes before chicken is done, add apricot mixture to tagine. Discard herbs and cinnamon stick, then serve chicken sprinkled with almonds on top.

Servings: 4

Total Time: 90 minutes

Chicken Tagine with Apricots and Spiced Pine Nuts

* 1 whole chicken (about 3 1/2 pound)
* 2 tablespoons extra-virgin olive oil, divided
* 3 large shallots, finely chopped (1 cup)
* 1 tablespoon unsalted butter
* 2 garlic cloves, minced
* 1 tablespoon grated peeled ginger
* 1/4 teaspoon turmeric
* 1/4 teaspoon sweet paprika
* Pinch of saffron threads (optional)
* 1 cup water
* 2 tablespoons blood-orange preserves or bitter-orange marmalade
* 1 (2-inch) cinnamon stick
* 1 thyme sprig
* 2 cilantro sprigs
* 6 dried apricots, chopped
* 1 tablespoon finely chopped cilantro or flat-leaf parsley

For spiced pine nuts
* 1 tablespoon olive oil
* 1/4 cup pine nuts
* 1/4 teaspoon turmeric
* 1/4 teaspoon sweet paprika
* Pinch of cayenne (optional)
* Garnish: lemon wedges

Procedure

1 Make tagine:

2 Cut out and reserve wings and backbone from chicken. Cut breast in half through bone, then cut off legs and cut to separate into thighs and drumsticks (for a total of 6 serving pieces, not including wings and backbone). Pat chicken pieces dry and sprinkle with 1 teaspoon salt.

3 Heat 1 tablespoon oil in a 12-inch heavy skillet over medium heat until it shimmers, then brown chicken breasts, skin sides down, without turning, 5 minutes. Transfer to a plate. Brown thighs and legs, turning once, 8 to 10 minutes, transferring to plate. Brown wings and backbone in same manner.

4 Cook shallots in butter with remaining tablespoon oil in a 5-
to 6-quart heavy pot over medium heat, stirring frequently,
until soft, 8 to 10 minutes. Add garlic, ginger, turmeric, and
paprika and cook, stirring, 3 minutes.

5 Add chicken with any juices from plate, saffron (if using), and
1/2 teaspoon salt to shallot mixture and turn chicken to coat.
Add water and bring to a boil, covered, then cook at a bare
simmer, covered, 30 minutes.

6 Turn chicken and add orange preserves, cinnamon stick,
thyme, cilantro sprigs, and apricots. Simmer, covered, 10
minutes. Uncover and simmer until chicken is very tender, 10
to 15 minutes more.

7 Brown pine nuts while chicken cooks:

8 Heat oil in a small heavy skillet over medium heat until it
shimmers, then stir in pine nuts, turmeric, paprika, and
cayenne (if using) and cook, stirring frequently, until nuts are
lightly browned, 1 to 2 minutes (watch carefully; they burn
easily). Transfer to a small bowl.

9 To serve:

10   Transfer chicken to a platter and keep warm, covered. If
sauce is not thick, boil, stirring occasionally, until reduced to
about 1 cup. Discard herb sprigs, cinnamon stick, wings, and
backbone. Stir in chopped cilantro and spoon sauce over
chicken. Sprinkle with nuts.

Servings: 4

Total Time: 120 minutes

Chicken Tagine with Green Olives

Chicken, lemon and green olives are a classic Moroccan flavor combination. Serve over Herbed Couscous with Tomatoes or Brown Rice & Greens.

12		bone-in chicken thighs (3 1/2-4 pounds), skin and fat removed
		Salt & coarsely ground pepper to taste
2	Tbs	extra-virgin olive oil, divided
1		large onion, thinly sliced
3		cloves garlic, finely chopped
1	Tbs	finely chopped fresh ginger
2	tsp	finely chopped fresh red or green chile pepper
4	cups	reduced-sodium chicken broth
2		all-purpose potatoes (8 ounces), peeled and diced
1/2 cup		large green olives, pitted and coarsely chopped
2	Tbs	lemon juice
1	Tbs	chopped fresh thyme or 1 teaspoon dried
1	Tbs	ground cumin
1	Tbs	ground cinnamon
1	tsp	turmeric
1	tsp	paprika
1/2 cup		chopped fresh cilantro

Procedure

1 Pat chicken dry and season with salt and pepper. Heat 1 tablespoon oil in a large ovenproof skillet or Dutch oven over medium-high heat until hot but not smoking. Add the chicken thighs (in batches if necessary) and cook, moving them around every couple of minutes, until browned on all sides, 5 to 7 minutes. Remove from the pan and set aside. Pour off fat.

2 Reduce heat to medium and add the remaining 1 tablespoon oil to the pan. Add onion and cook, stirring frequently, until they begin to brown, 5 to 7 minutes. Add garlic, ginger and chiles and cook for 2 minutes longer. Add broth, potatoes, olives, lemon juice, thyme, cumin, cinnamon, turmeric, paprika and the reserved chicken. Bring to a simmer.

3 Cover the pan, transfer it to the oven, and bake until the chicken thighs are tender, 45 minutes. Stir in cilantro. Season with salt and pepper and serve.

Servings: 6

Chicken Tagine with Lemon & Olives

1		chicken, about 3 lb.
2	Tbs	tagine spices
2		bay leaves
4	Tbs	extra-virgin olive oil
4		garlic cloves, sliced
		Salt and freshly ground pepper, to taste
2		small yellow onions, thinly sliced
1/2 cup		chopped fresh flat-leaf parsley,

plus more for garnish
1/2 cup chopped fresh cilantro
1/4 cup fresh lemon juice
6 preserved lemon wedges, rinsed and pulp removed, or peel of 1 lemon, cut into strips 1 inch long
1 cup green or black olives
Cooked couscous or basmati rice for serving

Procedure

1 Cut the chicken into serving pieces: 2 legs, 2 thighs and 2 wings; cut each half-breast in half. Set aside.

2 In a small sauté pan over medium heat, toast the spices, stirring frequently, until fragrant, about 3 minutes. Transfer to a large bowl. Add the bay leaves, 2 Tbs. of the olive oil, the garlic, salt and pepper and whisk to combine. Add the chicken and stir to coat. Cover with plastic wrap and refrigerate for 3 hours.

3 Remove the chicken from the marinade and reserve the marinade.

4 In a tagine or Dutch oven over medium-high heat, warm the remaining 2 Tbs. oil until almost smoking. Working in batches, brown the chicken on all sides, 5 to 7 minutes total. Transfer to a plate.

5 Add the onions to the tagine and cook, stirring, until soft and translucent, about 5 minutes. Reduce the heat to medium and add the chicken, reserved marinade, the 1/2 cup parsley, cilantro, lemon juice, preserved lemon and olives.

6 Cover the tagine and cook until the chicken is tender and falling off the bone, 1 to 1 1/2 hours. Discard the bay leaves.

Garnish with parsley and serve the chicken directly from the tagine. Accompany with couscous.

Servings: 6

Chicken Tagine with Lemons

2	Tbs	warm water	1	tsp	salt -- or less
1	pinch	saffron threads -- see note	8		large black olives -- see note
3	lbs	chicken -- cut into pieces	1		lemon zest -- fine julliened
2	Tbs	virgin olive oil	1		lemon slices -- cut 1/4" thick
2	tsp	margarine -- or butter			
1 1/2	cups	lowfat chicken broth			
1		small onion			
2	tsp	garlic -- finely chopped			
1	tsp	fresh ginger -- finely chopped			

- Place the water in a small bowl, add the saffron and soak for 10 minutes.

- Remove the skin from the SIX chicken pieces

Procedure

1 Place the water in a small bowl, add the saffron and soak for 10 minutes. Remove the skin from the SIX chicken pieces Place the chicken, oil, margarine, broth, onion, garlic, ginger and salt in a large saucepan, cover and bring to a boil over medium-high heat. Reduce the heat to low and cook, occasionally spooning the liquid over the chicken, until it is cooked through and the juices run clear when the chicken is tested with a skewer, about 40 to 45 minutes. Remove the onion and discard. Add the olives (see note) and lemon zest to the saucepan and simmer, uncovered, for an additionl 5 minutes. Place the chicken in a deep serving dish, pour the cooking juices on top and garnish

Servings: 6

Preparation Time: 15 minutes
Cooking Time: 60 minutes

Chicken Tagine with Olives and Preserved Lemons

1/4 cup	olive oil		1/4 tsp	saffron threads -- crumbled
2 3 lb	chickens -- each cut in 6 pieces		2	med tomatoes, peeled -- seeded and chopped
1/2 tsp	salt		6	cloves garlic -- finely chopped
1/4 tsp	freshly ground pepper			
2	sm onions -- finely chopped		1	cup fresh flat-leaf parsley -- finely chopped
1/4 tsp	ground ginger		1	cup fresh cilantro -- finely chopped
1	3" stick cinnamon		3	preserved lemons
			1/2 lb	mediterranean brine-cured olives -- calamata/picholine

Procedure

1 Heat the oil in a large enameled cast-iron casserole. Season the chicken pieces with the salt and pepper and add them to the casserole along with the onion, ginger, cinnamon, and saffron. Cook over high heat, turning the chicken occasionally, until browned all over, about 10 min. Add the tomatoes, garlic, parsley, cilantro and 2 c. of water and bring to a boil. Reduce the heat to low, cover and simmer, stirring occasionally, until the chicken is tender, about 1 hour. (The recipe can be prepared up to this point up to 2 days ahead; cover and refrigerate. Rewarm before continuing.)
Meanwhile, rinse the preserved lemons under running water; pat dry. Separate the lemons into quarters. Discard the pulp from one of the lemons and finely chop the peel. Reserve the quarters for garnish. Transfer the chicken to a large plate. Strain the cooking liquid and return it to the casserole. Boil over high heat until slightly thickened, about 10 min. Add the chopped preserved lemon and the olives and simmer over moderate heat for 2 min. Add the chicken pieces and simmer until heated through. Arrange the chicken pieces in a serving

Servings: 6

Chicken Tagine with Olives and Roast Peppers

Tagine is a classic Moroccan dish that takes its name from the uniquely shaped vessel in which it is cooked. The conical lid is designed to trap juices as they evaporate, causing them to condense and trickle back into the stew, keeping it moist and tender. The cooking process is intended to be slow; allowing for less expensive and less tender cuts of meat to be used. Traditionally, the tagine has been made of earthenware and was designed to be cooked over a wood fire and sometimes covered with hot coals. A modern version made from enameled cast iron, allows for this dish to be prepared on the stovetop.

1 1/2 cups	chopped onion, white or yellow
4		cloves garlic, minced
1	Tbs	olive oil
1 1/2 lbs		boneless, skinless chicken breast, cut into 1 1/2 pieces
1	Tbs	cumin
1	tsp	ground ginger
		A few saffron threads
1	tsp	ground white pepper
14		1/2-ounces fat free chicken stock
3		bell peppers (preferably 1 green, 1 red, 1 yellow) roasted, peeled, seeded and diced

2		carrots, peeled halved and roasted* and sliced in 1/2 slices
1		preserved lemon, skin only, diced
1	cup	pitted small green olives (you may want to omit these if you are watching your sodium intake)
1/2 cup		chopped cilantro
		Other necessary recipes: Preserved Lemons

Procedure

1 Saute onion in olive oil until softened but not browned. Add garlic and saute but do not brown.

2 Add chicken pieces which have been tossed in mixture of the spices. If time permits, toss chicken in this "dry rub" the night before to allow the flavors to permeate.

3 Cook the chicken/spice mixture over medium heat for approximately five minutes. If it starts to stick, add 1 tablespoon juice from the preserved lemons.

4 Pour in the stock and bring to a boil. Reduce to simmer and add the peppers, carrots, and lemon. Cover. Simmer for 4-5 minutes and stir in cilantro.

5 *Place carrots on sheet pan spray them lightly with canola or olive spray. Place pan in 425 degrees Fahrenheit oven and roast approximately 12 minutes or until carrots just begin to brown. Remove, cool and slice.

6 VARIATION:

7 Vegetarian variation of this can be made by substituting vegetable stock for chicken stock. The chicken can be omitted and 3 cups frozen artichoke hearts (thawed) can be added after sautéing the onion and garlic with spices.

Servings: 6

Total Time: 40 minutes

Chicken Tagine with Seven Vegetables

3 1/2 lb	Chicken
1	Tbs	Olive oil
1 3/4 lb	Eggplant
2	Tbs	Olive oil
1	cup	Onions, chopped
3		Garlic cloves, crushed
3	cup	Stock, chicken
1 1/2		Cinnamon sticks
1	tsp	Curry powder
1	tsp	Cumin, ground

1/4 tsp	Turmeric
1/4 tsp	Black pepper
1		Turnips
1		md Zucchini
1		Carrots
1/2		Bell peppers, red
3		md Tomatoes
1/2 cup	Raisins
1	Tbs	Parsley

Procedure

1 Cut chicken into serving pieces. Remove backs and wings and save for soup. Remove all skin and fat from chicken. Heat oil in large frying pan; saute chicken in 2 batches until opaque on both sides (a few minutes). Set aside.

2 Cut unpeeled eggplant into 1" cubes; salt for 20 minutes, then drain and rinse. Heat oil in 6-8-qt Dutch oven. Add onion, garlic, and eggplant. Saute over low heat until onion is just tender, 5-10 minutes.

3 Add stock, cinnamon, curry powder, cumin, turmeric, and black pepper. Stir, bring to boil, reduce heat, and simmer 10 minutes.

4 Peel turnip; dice turnip, zucchini, carrot, and bell pepper. Add dark meat and diced vegetables to Dutch oven. Simmer, uncovered, 10 minutes.

5 Dice tomatoes. Add chicken breasts, tomato, raisins, and parsley, pushing down lightly to be sure ingredients are covered by liquid. Simmer, covered, for 10 minutes more.

6 Serve hot in deep soup bowls on top of rice, noodles, or couscous, garnishing top with coriander.

Servings: 4

Recipe Tips

I used a whole chicken and dumped everything in the crockpot, which worked fine except that the vegetables weren't done (since it cooked about 6 hours instead of the usual 10 when I use the cp on a workday), so I boiled the vegetables in the stock until they were soft. However, I was not pleased with the result, and I think it was the combination of flavors (or lack thereof) rather than the cooking method. The chicken was fine, and the broth was delicious, but the vegetables were tasteless cardboard.

Chicken Tagine with Spring Vegetables

* 1 lemon, halved
* 6 medium artichokes, stems trimmed to 1/2 inch
* 1/2 cup (about) olive oil
* 1 pound onions, chopped
* 8 large garlic cloves, chopped
* 3 tablespoons (packed) grated lemon peel
* 1 tablespoon ground coriander
* 2 teaspoons Hungarian sweet paprika
* 1 1/2 teaspoons ground cumin
* 1 1/2 teaspoons ground ginger
* 1/4 teaspoon cayenne pepper
* 8 tablespoons chopped fresh parsley
* 8 tablespoons chopped fresh dill
* 8 tablespoons chopped fresh mint
* 4 pounds skinless boneless chicken thighs, trimmed of excess fat
* 4 cups low-salt chicken broth
* 3 fresh fennel bulbs, trimmed, bulbs quartered vertically
* 5 large carrots (about 1 1/2 pounds), peeled, cut into 1-inch lengths

Procedure

1 Fill large bowl with water; squeeze in juice from lemon. Working with 1 artichoke at a time, break off enough outer leaves to expose pale green leaves. Trim dark green areas off stem and base. Quarter artichoke lengthwise; trim artichoke quarters to 1 1/2-inch lengths. Scrape out choke; drop quarters into lemon water.

2 Heat 1/4 cup oil in heavy large skillet over medium-high heat. Add onions and sauté until translucent, about 5 minutes. Add next 7 ingredients and 6 tablespoons each parsley, dill, and mint; sauté 3 minutes longer. Scrape contents of skillet into heavy large pot; reserve skillet.

3 Sprinkle chicken with salt and pepper. Heat 2 tablespoons oil in same skillet over medium-high heat. Add 1/3 of chicken

and sauté until golden, about 3 minutes per side. Transfer to pot with onion mixture. Repeat with remaining chicken in 2 more batches, adding more oil by tablespoonfuls if needed. Add broth to skillet; bring to boil, scraping up browned bits. Transfer broth to pot; add fennel and carrots. Drain artichokes and add to pot.

4 Bring tagine to boil. Cover, reduce heat to medium-low, and simmer until chicken is almost tender, about 20 minutes. Uncover and simmer until chicken and all vegetables are tender, about 15 minutes longer. Using slotted spoon, transfer chicken and vegetables to large bowl. Boil sauce until reduced enough to coat spoon, about 10 minutes. Season with salt and pepper. Return chicken and vegetables to sauce. (Can be made 1 day ahead. Cool slightly. Chill uncovered until cold, then cover and keep refrigerated.)

5 Rewarm tagine over medium heat. Transfer to large bowl. Sprinkle with 2 tablespoons each of parsley, dill, and mint.

Servings: 8

Chicken With Candied Pumpkin - {Djaj Bel-Qera Mderbela}

The bird is a chicken, cooked as a Moroccan stew (tajine) instead of being roasted, but this dish has a curious similarity to the Thanksgiving combination of turkey and candied yams.

1	cup	62g / 2.2oz Coarsely-chopped onion	1		Chicken - (3 1/2 to 4 lbs)
1/4	tsp	1.3ml Ground ginger	1		Pumpkin or butternut squash - (3 lbs)
1/4	tsp	1.3ml Ground saffron	5	Tbs	75ml Butter
1	tsp	5ml Salt - divided	2	Tbs	30ml Honey
1	cup	237ml Olive oil	1/4 tsp		1.3ml Cinnamon
2 1/2	cups	592ml Water - divided			

Procedure

1 Place the onion, ginger, saffron, 1/2 teaspoon of salt, the oil and 2 cups of water in a food processor and process to a smooth liquid.

2 Place the liquid in a saucepan just large enough to hold the chicken, lay the chicken in it, cover and cook over medium heat until very tender and the meat is falling off the bone, 1 hour, 15 minutes to 1 hour, 30 minutes. From time to time, remove the lid and baste the chicken with the sauce. Add more water if the sauce is in danger of drying up.

3 Meanwhile, peel and seed the pumpkin or squash and cut it into 1-inch pieces. Place the pieces in a large skillet with 1/2 cup of water and the butter. Sprinkle with the remaining 1/2 teaspoon of salt. Simmer over low heat until very tender, 40 to 50 minutes.

4 Remove the squash from the skillet, place it in the food processor with the honey and cinnamon and process to a puree.

5 Serve the chicken in the sauce or with it on the side. Serve the pumpkin puree on the side or mix it into the sauce.

Servings: 4

Chicken with Cinnamon and Dates

1	Tbs	olive oil, plus 2 teaspoons
1/2	lb	(about 2 links) merguez, spicy Italian or lamb sausage, cut in halves or thirds (casings removed, if desired)
6 to 8		skinless chicken thighs
1 1/4	tsp	salt
3/4	tsp	freshly ground black pepper
2		large onions, thinly sliced
1	Tbs	white wine, orange juice or water
3		garlic cloves, smashed and coarsely chopped
1	Tbs	grated fresh ginger
1	tsp	ground cinnamon
1/2	tsp	ground cumin
1/2	tsp	hot paprika
1 1/2	cups	low-sodium chicken broth or water
1/2	cup	fresh orange juice
		About 1/3 cup golden raisins or currants
2 to 3		carrots, cut lengthwise and halved diagonally
12 to 15		pitted dates
1		large orange, cut into 8 wedges
2 to 3	Tbs	chopped fresh cilantro, plus additional for garnish
		Pine nuts, for garnish.

Procedure

1 Preheat oven to 350 degrees. Place a large Dutch oven (or skillet, if planning to bake in a tagine) over medium-high heat, and add 1 tablespoon olive oil. Add sausage and chicken, and sprinkle with half the salt and pepper. Brown about 5 minutes. Turn, sprinkle with remaining salt and pepper, and brown again about 5 minutes. Transfer to a plate or the bottom of a tagine.

2 Add 1 or 2 teaspoons olive oil to Dutch oven or skillet, as needed, and add onions. Sauté until onions are softened, about 5 minutes. Add wine, and stir, scraping bottom of pan. Add garlic, ginger, cinnamon, cumin and paprika, and stir

until garlic and ginger are softened and fragrant, about 3 minutes. Stir in chicken broth, orange juice, raisins and carrots. Return chicken and sausage to pot, or pour onion-carrot mixture over the chicken and sausage in tagine. Add dates and orange wedges, and stir to mix.

3 Cover, and bake until chicken and carrots are fork-tender, about 1 1/2 hours. Taste, and adjust seasonings as needed. Garnish with cilantro and pine nuts. If desired, serve with hot buttered couscous and harissa paste, or chutney.

Servings: 6

Cranberry duck tagine

2 Tbs unsalted whole cashews , lightly toasted

300g small parsnips , peeled and halved lengthways

1 tsp each ground ginger , coriander and cumin

3 large onions , thickly sliced

280g couscous

handfuls fresh or frozen whole cranberry (about 100g/4oz)

2 Tbs cranberry jelly

1 tsp plus 1 tbsp caster sugar

handful fresh mint leaves

1.2l hot chicken stock

sticks cinnamon or cassia bark

4 duck legs

strips orange zest , peeled off with a vegetable peeler

1 tsp ground cinnamon

1 Tbs sunflower or olive oil

Procedure

1 Preheat the oven to 190C/ gas 5/fan 170C. Put the duck legs in a shallow roasting tin and rub with salt, pepper, ground cinnamon and the oil. Roast for 25 minutes. Heat the cranberry jelly until thick and syrupy, then brush all over the duck and return to the oven for 20 minutes, until burnished and mahogany brown.

2 Put the onions and parsnips on the bottom of a heavybased shallow casserole and sit the duck on top. Sprinkle the spices and 1 tsp sugar over the duck and tuck the orange zest and cinnamon sticks around. Pour over 600ml/1 pint of the stock, so the duck sits in a shallow puddle. Cover and bring to a bubble on the hob, place in the oven and leave to murmur away for 1 hour. Add the cashews, cranberries and 1 tbsp sugar and cook for a further 30 minutes, uncovered, to let the duck skin crisp up.

3 Meanwhile, to prepare the couscous, tip into a heatproof bowl. Pour over the remaining 600ml/1 pint of stock. Leave for a minute or two, then fork it through. Leave for 4 minutes, then fluff through with a fork, with extra seasoning.

4 To serve, pile the couscous on to a plate and top with a duck leg, some vegetables, nuts and fruits, then spoon over the rich juices from the pan and scatter with mint. Or, if you make in advance, simply reheat for 30 minutes in a moderate oven.

Servings: 4

Cuisine from Morocco

And here for the fun of it, see if you can work it out - a Moroccan recipe in French

1	kg	de jarret de veau
2	kg	de petits pois frais
2		oignons
1/2		cuillère à café de safran
1		cuillère à café de piment doux

1	cuillère à café de sucre
3	cuillères à soupe d'huile d'arachide
2	citrons confits
	sel
	poivre

Procedure

1 Découper le veau et le mettre dans un faitout.

2 Ajouter le safran, le piment doux, les oignons coupés en morceaux, l'huile, le sel et le poivre.

3 Couvrir d'eau froide. Porter à ébullition et faire cuire à petit feu pendant 1 heure.

4 Retirer la viande. Mettre les petits pois dans le faitout, ajouter le sucre en poudre et faire cuire dans le bouillon pendant 20 minutes. Ajouter l'eau si nécessaire.

5 Retirer les petits pois. Couper l'écorce des citrons confits et les mettre dans le bouillon.

6 Faire réduire jusqu'à obtenir une sauce onctueuse.

7 Dresser la viande et les petits pois dans un tajine. Arroser de sauce et décorer avec les écorces de citrons.

8 Mettre la plat à chauffer quelques minutes sur feux doux avant de servir.

Servings: 4

Fatima's chicken tagine with cous cous

4		Large chicken thighs	4		Large chicken thighs
1		onion, chopped	1		onion, chopped
4	Tbs	oil	4	Tbs	oil
1	Tbs	salt	1	Tbs	salt
1	tsp	ginger	1	tsp	ginger
1/4 tsp		saffron	1/4 tsp		saffron
1/2 tsp		cinnamon	1/2 tsp		cinnamon
2		tomatoes, chopped	2		tomatoes, chopped
3		carrots, chopped into large batons	3		carrots, chopped into large batons
2		parsnips, chopped into large batons	2		parsnips, chopped into large batons
2		courgettes, chopped into large batons	2		courgettes, chopped into large batons
1		aubergine, roughly sliced	1		aubergine, roughly sliced
1		small cabbage, roughly chopped	1		small cabbage, roughly chopped
1/2 kg		cous cous	1/2 kg		cous cous

Procedure

1 heat a large pressure cooker/ slow cooker
2 add 4 tablespoons of oil and the chopped onion into the cooker pan.
3 fry the onion in the oil.
4 add the chicken thighs to the pan
5 add the salt, ginger, saffron, cinnamon and stir the ingredients together.
6 add the lid and leave to cook until the chicken turns white in colour
7 add all the vegetables to the pan.

8 add boiling water to the pan so that it just covers the top of the vegetables (about 1/2 to 3/4 the way to the top of the pan)

9 put the pan on a moderate heat and cover with the lid. Leave to cook for 45 minutes.

10   clean the cous cous in cold water, add salt and drain the water from the cous cous.

11   leave the wet cous cous in a bowl until it dries

12   using a cous cous pan/ 2 tier steamer, put 1 pint of water on the hob to boil

13   when the cous cous has dried add a little drop of oil and mix in to stop the cous cous from sticking together

14   once the water has started to boil, add the cous cous to the top section of the pan, place on top of the pan with boiling water and leave for 25 -30 minutes to cook

15   once the cous cous has cooked (it will expand and soften but shouldn't be soggy)take off the heat and stir the cous cous in a bowl.

16   transfer the cous cous to a tagine plate. pour over the jus/gravy from the cooked chicken and vegetables. make a hole in the centre of the cous cous and add the chicken and vegetables.

Servings: 4

Fish Tagine

Swordfish with a tantalizing blend of herbs served over a bed of couscous.

1	lb	swordfish fillets (or use scrod or sea bass)	4 tsp	ground cumin
1		medium onions, thinly sliced	1 cup	fresh lemon juice (6 to 8 lemons)
1		fresh carrots, thinly sliced	1	red hot chile peppers, minced, seeds removed
1/2 tsp		salt	2	large tomato, chopped
1	cup	fresh cilantro, chopped	1 pinch	salt
10		medium garlic cloves, minced or pressed	1 cup	Couscous, cooked
2	Tbs	fresh ginger root, grated	1 Tbs	canola oil

Procedure

1 Preheat the oven to 350 degrees Fahrenheit.

2 Rinse the fish fillets and set them aside. Coat a casserole dish with oil. Arrange the onions and carrots in a layer to cover the bottom of the dish and place the fillets on top. Lightly sprinkle them with salt.

3 In a blender or food processor, combine the cilantro, garlic, ginger, cumin, lemon juice, chile, and half of the chopped tomatoes and puree to form a smooth sauce. Add salt to taste. Pour the sauce evenly over the fish and vegetables and top with the remaining chopped tomatoes.

4 Cover tightly with foil and bake for 20 to 25 minutes, until the fish flakes easily with a fork. Serve immediately on couscous.

Servings: 4

Author Notes

A tantalizing blend of garlic, cilantro, and cumin sparked by fresh ginger and fresh chile.

Fish Tagine with Preserved Lemon and Tomatoes

A tasty layered fish and vegetable casserole.

1		cooking spray
1		medium lemons, finely chopped
1	Tbs	water
1	Tbs	olive oil, divided
1	tsp	sugar
1/8 tsp		saffron, crushed
3	Tbs	chopped parsley
3	Tbs	fresh cilantro, chopped
3/4 tsp		Salt Substitute, no sodium

1/2	tsp	paprika, sweet, Hungarian
1/2	tsp	ground cumin
1/4	tsp	black pepper
12		Olives, green, manzanilla, stuffed, thinly sliced
2		medium garlic cloves, minced
1 1/2 lb		mahi mahi fillets
2	cup	sliced white onion
4	cup	chopped tomato, seeded
1	pinch	fresh cilantro (optional)

Procedure

1 Heat a small, cooking spray coated skillet over medium high heat.

2 Combine lemon, 1 tablespoon water, 1/2 teaspoon oil, and sugar in skillet and let cook for 3 minutes, stir occasionally, water will be absorbed and mixture will be slightly golden, reserve.

3 In a small microwave safe bowl, heat 2 1/2 teaspoons of oil in a microwave until warmed, 10 seconds at a time. Mix in saffron and let infuse 10 minutes.

4 In a large resealable plastic bag, mix lettuce, saffron oil, parsley, cilantro, salt, paprika, olives, and garlic. Place fish in bag, seal and chill for 30 minutes, flipping once or twice.

5 Preheat oven to 400 degrees F.

6 Grease a 13 by 9 inch baking pan with cooking spray.

7 Arrange 1 cup onion slices and 2 cups of tomatoes on the bottom of the pan.

8 Take fish out of bag, saving liquid, and lay fish on top of tomatoes. Spoon the liquid over the fish and top with the rest of the tomatoes and onions.

9 Wrap pan with aluminum foil and cook for 40 minutes or until preferred degree of doneness.

10   Take out of oven and move fish and vegetables to a serving dish. Spoon the liquid over the fish and scatter cilantro leaves over, if using.

Servings: 4

Author Notes

Any firm white fish such as mahi mahi, halibut, or sea bass will work with this recipe.

Fish Tagine with Tomatoes, Capers, and Cinnamon

* 3/4 teaspoon ground cumin
* 1/4 cup extra-virgin olive oil
* 1 (15-ounce) can stewed tomatoes, chopped
* 1 1/2 tablespoons drained capers
* 1/2 teaspoon cinnamon
* 4 (6-ounce) pieces hake or halibut fillet (about 1-inch-thick)

Procedure

1 Heat cumin in oil in a 12-inch heavy skillet over medium heat, stirring occasionally, until fragrant, about 1 minute. Stir in tomatoes, capers, cinnamon, and 1/4 teaspoon each of salt and pepper and simmer, uncovered, stirring occasionally, until thickened, about 10 minutes.

2 Pat fish dry and sprinkle with 1/4 teaspoon each of salt and pepper, then add to skillet. Cover and simmer until fish is just cooked through, 7 to 10 minutes.

Servings: 6

Total Time: 25 minutes

Lamb & Pear Tagine

Tagines are Moroccan slow-cooked meat, fruit & vegitable dishes which are almost invariablely made with mutton. Using lamb cuts down the cooking time, but if you can find good hogget (older than lamb, younger than mutton, commonly labelled "baking legs" and sold cheaply) that will do very well.

2		lg Onions, peeled & sliced
1	kg	Lean lamb, leg or shoulder cut into 4cm cubes.
4		Pears, peeled cored & cut into 4cm chunks
1/2 cup		Sultanas
1/2 cup		Silvered almonds
1	Tbs	Olive oil
1	tsp	Cumin

1 tsp Ground coriander
1 tsp Ground ginger
1 tsp Cinnamon
1 tsp Black pepper
Water, to cover the meat
Salt, to tast

Procedure

1 In a large saucepan gently fry the onion in the olive oil until soft, add the meat to the pan and cook until it changes color, then add the spices. Add water to just cover the meat and salt to taste. Cover and simmer gently until the meat is tender, about 1 1/2 - 2 hours. (Displace the lid a little after an hour if there appears to be too much liquid.)

2 Add the pears to the meat together with the sultanas & almonds. Cook for a further 5 minutes or until the pears are soft. Serve with rice.

Servings: 6

Lamb And Dried Fruit Tagine

1.50	tsp	Ginger	2.00		large Carrots; peeled, cut into 2
12.00		each Pitted prunes			
2.00	tsp	Minced garlic	2.00		medium Yukon Gold potatoes; peeled, Garnish:; optional
		Chopped cilantro or mint			
		Toasted blanched almonds	0.25	tsp	Saffron threads; optional
0.50	tsp	Cayenne pepper	12.00		each Dried apricots
2.00	Tbs	Fresh lemon juice	1.50	lb	Well-trimmed boneless lamb
1.00		each Cinnamon stick			
1.50	tsp	Ground cumin			Couscous
1.00	Tbs	Olive oil	1.50	cup	Sliced onion
3.00	cup	Chicken broth	1.50	tsp	Coriander
			0.50	tsp	Salt

Procedure

1 In Dutch oven, in oil, brown lamb in batches, 5 minutes per batch. Remove with slotted spoon.

2 Add onion and 1/4 cup broth. Cover; cook stirring occasionally, 8 minutes, until softened. Add garlic, cumin, coriander, ginger, cayenne and salt; cook, stirring, 1 minute.

3 Return meat and it's juices to pot. Add remaining broth, the cinnamon and saffron; simmer, covered, 1- 1/4 hours. Add potatoes and carrots; simmer covered, 15 minutes. Add apricots and prunes; simmer, uncovered 10 minutes, until lamb is tender and liquid has thickened. Discard cinnamon.

4 Add honey and lemon juice. Serve with couscous and garnish, if desired.

Servings: 4

Lamb and Prune Tagine Recipe

I just love this kind of stew -- the lamb and prunes make a wonderful combination (you could use apricots instead of the prunes if you prefer) and the slow cooking means the meat comes out tender everytime.

* 1 kg diced lamb, trimmed of most of its fat
* 1 large onion, peeled and sliced
* 1 teaspoon freshly ground white pepper
* 1 teaspoon cumin
* 1 teaspoon ginger
* 1 teaspoon nutmeg
* 1 pinch saffron
* 1 pinch salt
* 1 preserved lemon, chopped or 1/2 lemon, juice and zest of or 1 seville orange (optional)

* 12 dried prunes (you could also use apricots)
* 4 cloves garlic, peeled and chopped
* 2 tablespoons extra virgin olive oil
* 1/4 cup whole blanched almond, lightly toasted to serve
* chopped coriander, to serve

Procedure

1 Preheat the oven to 300F or 150 degrees C.
2 Put the meat in a tagine or other earthenware casserole.
3 Add the rest of the ingredients and put on the lid.
4 Seal this tightly with foil, or a flour and water paste, and cook in the very low oven for 2 1/2-3 hours.
5 As a variation, you could also make a soup by adding chickpeas, chopped onions, carrots, celery, turnips and plenty more water.

Servings: 6

Preparation Time: 10 minutes
Cooking Time: 0 minutes

Lamb Shallot And Date Tagine

1 1/2 kg		Leg of lamb; diced	1	Tbs	Olive oil
1	Tbs	Tomato puree	2	Tbs	Chopped coriander
2	tsp	Ground coriander	18		Shallots whole; peeled
1		Cinnamon stick			A preserved lemon; rind of
2	tsp	Ground ginger	4		Cloves garlic; crushed
600	ml	Lamb stock	4	oz	Pitted medjool dates
1	pinches	saffron	1	Tbs	Plain flour
2	Tbs	Chopped flat parsley	1	Tbs	Clear honey

Procedure

1 Put the lamb in a bowl and add the coriander, ginger, saffron and olive oil. Mix and marinade the lamb for 24 hours. Brown off the lamb. Set aside.

2 Fry the shallots until lightly golden and add the garlic and lamb. Add the plain flour, tomato puree and cinnamon stick. 3 Add the lamb stock and bring to the boil. Cover tightly and simmer gently for 1 1/2 hours. Add the chopped parsley, coriander, lemon rind, dates and honey.

Servings: 4

Lamb Tagine

"This is a traditional Moroccan lamb tagine simmered in numerous spices. Don't let the long ingredients list put you off. If you are missing one or two the dish will still turn out fine."

45	ml	olive oil, divided
905	g	lamb meat, cut into 1 1/2 inch cubes
5	g	paprika
0.6	g	ground turmeric
1	g	ground cumin
0.4	g	cayenne pepper
2	g	ground cinnamon
0.5	g	ground cloves
1	g	ground cardamom
5	g	kosher salt
0.9	g	ground ginger
1	g	saffron
2	g	garlic powder

2	g	ground coriander
220	g	onions, cut into 1-inch cubes
5		carrots, peeled, cut into fourths, then sliced lengthwise into thin strips
3		cloves garlic, minced
6	g	freshly grated ginger
1		lemon, zested
1		(14.5 ounce) can homemade chicken broth or low-sodium canned broth
20	g	sun-dried tomato paste
15	ml	honey
8	g	cornstarch (optional)
15	ml	water (optional)

Procedure

1 Place diced lamb in a bowl, toss with 2 tablespoons of the olive oil, and set aside. In a large resealable bag, toss together the paprika, turmeric, cumin, cayenne, cinnamon, cloves, cardamom, salt, ginger, saffron, garlic powder, and coriander; mix well. Add the lamb to the bag, and toss around to coat well. Refrigerate at least 8 hours, preferably overnight.

2 Heat 1 tablespoon of olive oil in a large, heavy bottomed pot over medium-high heat. Add 1/3 of the lamb, and brown well. Remove to a plate, and repeat with remaining lamb.

Add onions and carrots to the pot and cook for 5 minutes. Stir in the fresh garlic and ginger; continue cooking for an additional 5 minutes. Return the lamb to the pot and stir in the lemon zest, chicken broth, tomato paste, and honey. Bring to a boil, then reduce heat to low, cover, and simmer for 1 1/2 to 2 hours, stirring occasionally, until the meat is tender.

3 If the consistency of the tagine is too thin, you may thicken it with a mixture of cornstarch and water during the last 5 minutes.

Servings: 4

Preparation Time: 45 minutes
Cooking Time: 120 minutes
Total Time: 645 minutes

Lamb Tagine With Apricots, Olives and Buttered Almonds

4	lbs	bone-in lamb shoulder or neck, or 21/4 pounds boneless lamb stew meat, cut into 2-inch chunks
		4garlic cloves, minced
1		1/2teaspoons kosher salt
1	tsp	freshly ground black pepper
1	tsp	sweet paprika
1	tsp	ground ginger
3/4	tsp	ground cumin
2		large Spanish onions, peeled and quartered
2		cinnamon sticks, each 2 inches long
		Large pinch crumbled saffron
1 1/4 cups		dried apricots, sliced
1	cup	cracked green olives, pitted and sliced if desired
2 to 4Tbs		butter
1/3	cup	sliced almonds
		Cooked couscous, for serving
		Chopped parsley or cilantro, for

3. Place pot over high heat and let cook, turning meat on all sides, until spices release their scent, about 3 minutes. You need not brown meat. Add 3 cups water to pot (it should come 3/4 of the way up lamb), along with cinnamon and saffron. Bring to a s

4. Turn meat, then top with onion slices. Cover pot and braise for another 45 minutes to an hour, or until lamb is very tender. Use a slotted spoon to transfer meat to a bowl, leaving broth and onions in pot.

5. Place pot on stove over high heat and add 3/4 cup apricots and the olives. Simmer broth until it reduces by a third and thickens slightly, about 10 minutes. Return lamb to pot and keep warm until serving. (Tagine can be prepared 4 days ahead; chill, th

6. To serve, chop remaining 1/2 cup apricot slices. In a small skillet, melt butter. Add almonds and cook until well browned and toasted, about 2 minutes. Put couscous in a serving bowl

49

garnish.

1. Preheat oven to 325 degrees. Trim excess fat off lamb. Put meat in a deep Dutch oven or cast-iron pot with the garlic, salt, black pepper, paprika, ginger and cumin. Rub spices and garlic evenly all over meat.

2. Thinly slice onions, then mince enough of them to yield 1/2 cup. Add minced onion to pot with lamb; reserve onion slices.

and top with almonds and butter and chopped apricots. Pile tagine in

Servings: 6

Lamb Tagine with Artichokes and Mint

3	lb	(1.5 kg) boneless lamb shoulder or leg roast	1		bay leaf
			1/2 tsp		(2 mL) salt
			1/4 tsp		(1 mL) pepper
2	Tbs	(25 mL) olive oil	1		can (19 oz/540 mL) chickpeas, drained and rinsed
2		onions, sliced			
1		carrot, diced			
4		cloves garlic, minced	1		can (14 oz/398 mL) artichokes, drained and quartered
2	tsp	(10 mL) crumbled dried mint	1/4 cup		(50 mL) raisins
1	tsp	(5 mL) ground cumin	1	tsp	(5 mL) grated lemon rind
1/4	cup	(50 mL) dry white wine	1	Tbs	(15 mL) lemon juice
1-1/2	cups	(375 mL) chicken stock	1/4 cup		(50 mL) pine nuts

Procedure

1 Preheat oven to 350°F (180°C).

2 Trim roast and cut into 1-inch (2.5 cm) cubes. In large Dutch oven, heat oil over medium-high heat; brown lamb in batches. Transfer to plate.

3 Drain any fat from pan and reduce heat to medium; cook onions, carrot, garlic, mint and cumin, stirring, until onions are softened, about 5 minutes. Add wine; cook, stirring, for 1 minute. Add chicken stock, bay leaf, salt and pepper.

4 Return lamb and any accumulated juices to pan; bring to boil.

5 Cover and simmer over medium-low heat, or cover and cook in oven, for 1 hour.

6 Stir in chickpeas, artichokes, raisins and lemon rind and juice; cover and cook until lamb is tender and sauce is thickened, about 30 minutes. Discard bay leaf.

7 Meanwhile, in small skillet, toast pine nuts over medium heat, shaking often, until golden, about 3 minutes; sprinkle over stew.

Servings: 6

Lamb Tagine With Chickpeas And Raisins, Basmati Rice, Harissa

2	lbs	lamb shoulder, cut 2" pieces	2		red bell peppers, roasted, peeled, and chopped
6		garlic cloves, coarsely chopped	1		small red chile, chopped
1	Tbs	honey	2		garlic cloves, chopped
1/4	cup	olive oil	1/2		tea pon coriander seeds, toasted in a pan
3	Tbs	chopped cilantro			
1	pinch	saffron threads			
2	tsp	paprika	1/2	tsp	cumin
2	tsp	ground cumin			Salt, to taste
2	Tbs	sun-dried tomato paste	3	Tbs	olive oil
		Salt, to taste			=== BASMATI RICE ===
		Freshly-ground black pepper, to taste	2	Tbs	olive oil
2		potatoes, cut into chunks	1		yellow onion, finely chopped
2		carrots, cut into chunks	1	tsp	cumin seeds
2		yellow onions, peeled, and cut into chunks	1		cinnamon stick
			2		cardamom seeds, crushed
			2		bay leaves
1 1/2	cups	vegetable stock	2	cups	basmati rice, washed well, drained
1		cinnamon stick	3	cups	water
1	cup	cooked chickpeas	2	Tbs	lemon juice
1/2	cup	golden raisins			Salt, to taste
		=== HARISSA ===			Freshly-ground black pepper, to taste

Procedure

1 Tagine: Mix together the garlic, honey, olive oil, cilantro, saffron, paprika, cumin and tomato paste in a large bowl. Add

53

the lamb and toss to coat. Cover and marinate in the refrigerator overnight. Remove from the refrigerator 30 minutes before cooking.

2 Preheat oven to 400 degrees. Put the meat and the marinade into a tagine or Dutch oven and sprinkle with salt and pepper. Add the potatoes, carrots, onions, stock and cinnamon and stir together. Place the tagine or Dutch oven lid on and bake for 1 hour.

3 Stir the chickpeas and raisins into the tagine and cook for 30 minutes. Remove the lid or foil and cook an additional 30 minutes to brown the vegetables. Garnish with cilantro springs.

4 Harissa: Combine all ingredients in a food processor and process until smooth.

5 Basmati Rice: Heat oil in a medium saucepan over medium heat. Add the onions and cook until soft. Add the cumin seeds, cinnamon stick, cardamom seeds and bay leaves and cook for 2 to 3 minutes.

6 Add the rice and toss to coat with the mixture. Add the water and lemon juice and season with salt and pepper. Bring to a boil, cover and reduce heat to medium-low, cook for 15 minutes, or until rice is tender and water has been absorbed. Remove from the heat and leave covered for 5 minutes. Fluff with a fork.

Servings: 4

Lamb Tagine with Golden Raisins

This is a French Moroccan-inspired stew in which nuggets of lamb, redolent of cinnamon, are cooked until the meat is so tender it practically melts in your mouth. The raisins and the caramelized onion topping add a touch of sweetness, which is cut by the subtle acidity of tomato and the bright taste of fresh cilantro, stirred in at the last minute. This is best served with plain fluffy couscous.

1 lb	lamb stew meat (from the shoulder or leg)	2	Tbs	butter
1	clove garlic, smashed and peeled	2		sweet onions, halved and thinly sliced
2	tomatoes, chopped	1 1/2tsp		ground cumin
1 Tbs	good-quality ground cinnamon	3/4	cup	golden raisins
2 tsp	sugar	2	cups	instant couscous, cooked in lightly salted water and fluffed with a fork
	Salt and freshly ground pepper			
1 Tbs	tomato paste (optional; see tip)			
1	bunch fresh cilantro			

Procedure

1 Place the lamb in a 4-quart slow cooker and add the garlic, tomatoes, cinnamon, sugar, 1 teaspoon salt, 1/2 teaspoon pepper, 1/2 cup water and the tomato paste, if using. Keeping the cilantro in a bunch, cut off the stems and tie them together with kitchen strings; set the leaves aside. Nestle the bundle of stems into the ingredients in the slow cooker. Cook on the low setting for 5 to 6 hours, or until the lamb is very tender, then remove and discard the cilantro stems. Meanwhile, put the butter, onions and cumin in a medium skillet or saute pan and cook over low heat, stirring occasionally, until the onion is very soft and deep golden brown, about 30 minutes. Season with salt and pepper to taste, then remove from heat. Twenty minutes before the end of the cooking time for the lamb, remove the lid and

skim off as much of the clear fat from the surface of the stew as possible. Reserving a few sprigs for garnish, roughly chop the cilantro leaves and stir them, along with the raisins, into the lamb; continue to cook, uncovered, on the high setting, for 20 minutes. Taste and season with salt and pepper as necessary. Spoon the couscous onto a serving platter or individual plates and top with the lamb and the caramelized onion and reserved cilantro sprigs.

Servings: 4

Author Notes

Works best in a 4-quart slow cooker If the fresh tomato isn't top quality, ripe and red, use a little tomato paste to enhance the flavor of the tagine: Stir it into the water when you load the slow cooker.

Lamb Tagine With Honey, Prunes, Onions And Toasted

18		pearl onions, blanched, peeled	2	Tbs	honey
2	Tbs	olive oil	1	tsp	ground turmeric
4	lbs	lamb stew meat, cut 1" cubes	1/2	tsp	ground cinnamon
		= (or a whole 4 1/2-lb leg, cut	1/8	tsp	ground mace
		into 1" cubes, reserving bone)	16		pitted prunes - (abt 6 oz)
1		medium onion, finely diced			Salt, to taste
					Freshly-ground black pepper, to taste
10		Spanish saffron threads	1/2	cup	whole almonds, toasted
1 1/2	cups	homemade or canned beef stock			

Procedure

1 In a small saucepan filled with boiling water, blanch the pearl onions for 1 minute. Drain and let cool. Peel the onions and set aside.

2 In a 4-quart or larger pressure cooker, heat the olive oil over medium-high heat. Brown the meat in batches on all sides. Avoid overcrowding the meat or it will not brown properly. Transfer the meat to a platter.

3 Add the diced onions to the pan and cook, stirring occasionally, until softened.

4 Meanwhile, grind the saffron in a mortar and pestle (or rub it between your finger) and add it to the beef stock.

5 Return the meat to the pot. Stir in the saffron mixture along with any bones. Stir in the honey, turmeric, cinnamon, mace, and prunes.

6 Cover the cooker and bring pressure to the second red ring (15 pounds pressure) over high heat. Adjust heat downward

to maintain the pressure at the second red ring and cook 15 minutes.

7 Open the pressure cooker using fingertip Release Method and add the onions. Stir well.

8 Cover again and bring pressure up to the second red ring. Adjust heat downward to maintain the pressure at the second red ring and cook 5 minutes more. Use Natural Release Method.

9 Meanwhile, in a non-stick frypan, toast the almonds until golden. Set aside.

10 Remove the cover from the pressure cooker and strain off all fat. (A good way to do this is to pour off all the liquid into a fat skimmer and pour off all the juice, leaving the fat. Discard the fat.)

11 Use the non-stick pan you have used to toast the almonds to reduce the sauce until slightly thicker. (The wider pan quickens this process.) Taste and add salt and pepper as needed.

12 Return the sauce to the pot and sprinkle the stew with the almonds. Serve with couscous or rice in shallow bowls.

Servings: 6

Lamb Tagine with Prunes

1440		gm Lamb shanks, sawed into 1 -inch pieces	1	tsp	Olive oil
			2	tsp	Sugar
3		med Onions, one peeled and grated, two peeled and thickly sliced	0.5	cup	Canned crushed tomatoes
			1	cup	Canned chick-peas
			3	cup	Pumpkin or butternut squash chunks
3	tsp	Ras El Hanout, plus more to taste	0.75	cup	Pitted prunes, halved
		Salt & freshly ground pepper			Harissa Sauce (separate recipe follows)
1		tblsp Plus 1 t unsalted butter			Lavash or pita bread
		Large pinch of saffron			
3	cup	Water			
1		Cinnamon stick			

Procedure

1 Coat lamb with grated onion, ras el hanout, and salt and pepper. Marinate in refrigerator for 30 minutes or up to 2 hours. Melt 1 T butter in a wide, heavy-bottomed pan. Add meat and brown lightly on all sides. Add saffron, water, and cinnamon stick; bring to a boil. Reduce heat to a simmer and cook, covered, for 1 1/2 hours.

2 Let cool slightly and remove shanks. Pull meat from bones, keeping pieces as large as possible; discard fat, gristle, and bones. Season with salt and pepper. Skim fat from liquid, or refrigerate overnight and remove fat. Refrigerate meat.

3 In a medium saute pan, heat 1 t butter and 1 t oil. Add sliced onions and sprinkle with sugar and salt and pepper to taste. Cook over medium-high heat for 15 minutes, tossing or stirring only when brown. Turn heat to low and cook until onions are very soft and brown, about 10 more minutes.

4 Add tomatoes and cooking liquid from the lamb and bring to a boil. Add meat, chick-peas, and pumpkin or squash and

simmer, covered, for 15 minutes. Remove lid, stir in prunes, and simmer until thick, about 15 to 20 more minutes. Adjust seasonings to taste. Serve immediately with harissa sauce and lavash or pita bread.

Servings: 4

Lamb Tagine with Prunes and Cinnamon Gourmet

This well-balanced stew is intense yet mellow. The prunes soak up the fragrant spices, and long, slow cooking turns the lamb fork-tender.

2 1/2 lb		boneless lamb shoulder, cut into 1 1/2-inch pieces
1		medium red onion, halved and thinly sliced
3	Tbs	plus 1/4 cup olive oil, divided
3		(3-inch) cinnamon sticks
1	tsp	ground cinnamon
1	tsp	ground ginger
1	tsp	turmeric
1		pinch saffron threads

1	Tbs	white wine or water
		About 2 1/2 cups water
1/2 lb		prunes (about 2 cups)
3	Tbs	mild honey
1	Tbs	sesame seeds
1/2 cup		whole blanched almonds
		preparation

Procedure

1 Toss together lamb, onion, 3 tablespoons oil, spices (except saffron), 1 teaspoon salt, and 1/2 teaspoon pepper in a 5- to 6-quart heavy pot.

2 Lightly toast saffron in a dry small skillet (not nonstick) over medium heat until just fragrant, 15 to 30 seconds. Crumble into wine and let stand 1 minute. Add wine to pot, then add enough water to just cover lamb. Gently simmer, partially covered, stirring occasionally, 1 1/2 hours.

3 Stir in prunes and honey and simmer until meat is tender and sauce has thickened, 15 to 20 minutes. Season with salt.

4 Toast sesame seeds in dry small skillet over medium heat, stirring, until pale golden, then transfer to a small bowl.

5 Heat remaining 1/4 cup oil in same skillet over medium-high heat until it shimmers, then fry almonds until golden. Drain

on paper towels. Serve tagine sprinkled with sesame seeds and almonds.

Servings: 6

Author Notes

Tagine can be cooked 1 day ahead and chilled (covered once cool). Reheat gently, thinning with water if needed.

Lamb Tagine With Prunes, Apricots, And Vegetables

2	lbs	lamb shoulder chops, 1" thick
1	Tbs	vegetable oil, divided
1		large onion, chopped
1 1/2	cups	water
1	pinch	saffron threads, crumbled
3/4	tsp	salt
1/4	tsp	freshly-ground black pepper
1 1/2		large carrots, cut 1/4"-thk rounds
1		small sweet potato, peeled, and

		cut into 3/4" pieces
3/4	tsp	ground ginger
1/8	tsp	ground cinnamon
2/3	cup	pitted prunes
1/2	cup	dried apricots
1		medium yellow squash, cut 3/4" pieces
2	tsp	honey, (optional)
		Freshly-grated nutmeg, to taste

Procedure

1 Cut lamb from bones, reserving bones, then cut meat into 1-inch pieces.

2 Heat 1/2 tablespoon of the oil in a flameproof wide shallow casserole with a tight-fitting lid over moderately-high heat until hot but not smoking. Brown meat on all sides in 2 batches, transferring to a plate as browned. Brown bones and transfer to plate.

3 Add remaining 1/2 tablespoon oil to the casserole and cook onion, stirring, until softened. Return meat and bones to pot. Stir in water, saffron, salt, and pepper and bring to a boil. Reduce heat and simmer mixture, covered, stirring occasionally, until lamb is tender, about 1 1/4 hours.

4 Transfer the lamb to a clean plate and add any meat from lamb bones, discarding bones. Add carrots and sweet potato to pot, then simmer, covered, stirring occasionally, until vegetables are barely tender, about 10 minutes.

5 Add ginger, cinnamon, prunes, apricots, and squash, simmer, covered, stirring occasionally, until vegetables and fruits are tender, about 5 minutes. Return lamb to stew and add honey. Season with salt, pepper, and nutmeg and simmer, uncovered, stirring occasionally, 5 minutes.

Servings: 4

Lamb Tagine with Tomatoes and Caramelized Sweet Onions

* 9 cups chopped sweet onions (such as Vidalia or Maui; about 3 pounds), divided
* 3 pounds boneless lamb stew meat, cut into 3/4- to 1-inch pieces
* 2 cups water
* 2 cinnamon sticks
* 1 teaspoon ground cinnamon
* 1 teaspoon salt
* 1 teaspoon coarsely ground black pepper
* 1 teaspoon ground ginger
* 1/8 teaspoon crumbled saffron threads
* 4 cups chopped plum tomatoes (about 1 1/2 pounds)
* 4 tablespoons chopped fresh Italian parsley, divided
* 1/4 cup olive oil

Procedure

1 Combine 3 cups chopped onions, lamb, and 2 cups water in heavy large pot. Add cinnamon sticks, ground cinnamon, salt, pepper, ginger, and saffron; bring to boil over medium-high heat. Partially cover, reduce heat to medium-low, and simmer gently 1 1/2 hours. Add tomatoes and 2 tablespoons parsley. Continue to simmer, partially covered, until lamb is tender and juices thicken, about 30 minutes. Season to taste with salt and pepper. Remove cinnamon sticks.

2 Meanwhile, heat oil in heavy large skillet over high heat. Add remaining 6 cups chopped onions. Sauté until beginning to brown, about 10 minutes. Reduce heat to medium; sauté until onions are deep brown, stirring often, about 45 minutes. DO AHEAD: Stew and onions can be made 1 day ahead. Cool, cover, and chill separately. Rewarm each over low heat before continuing.

3 Transfer lamb stew to large shallow bowl. Scatter caramelized onions and remaining 2 tablespoons parsley over.

Servings: 6

Lamb Tajine With Dates & Almonds

1.00	tsp	Ground cinnamon
0.50	tsp	Powdered saffron
200.00	g	Blanched almonds toasted
30.00	g	Butter cut in pieces
2.00		each Spanish onions finely chppd
2.00	tsp	Lemon juice
40.00	g	Fresh dates pitted
1.00	Tbs	Sesame seeds toasted
12.00		each Lamb cutlets trimmed of fat
0.50	tsp	Freshly ground black pepper
2.00	Tbs	Honey
2.00	Tbs	Freshly chopped coriander

Procedure

1 Place cutlets in a greased tagine or ovenproof casserole. Add pepper, saffron, onion, butter, salt to taste and enough water to cover. Bring slowly to the boil, cover and simmer for 1.1/2 - 2 hours, or until lamb is tender, occasionally skimming any fat from the surface.

2 Add the honey, cinnamon and coriander and cook for 5 mins longer, turning meat. Remove the cutlets from the dish with a slotted spoon and keep warm.

3 Add lemon juice to sauce and season to taste with salt and freshly ground black pepper.

4 Add dates and simmer, uncovered, for 10 mins, or until sauce is reduced and slightly thickened. Return meat to pan and cook until heated through. Sprinkle with almonds and sesame seeds.

Servings: 4

Lamb, Shallot and Date Tajine Recipe

3 1/4 lbs		leg of lamb, diced	1	Tbs	tomato puree
2	tsp	ground coriander	1		cinnamon stick
2	tsp	ground ginger	1	pint	lamb stock (or chicken stock)
1	pinch	saffron			
1	Tbs	olive oil	2	Tbs	chopped flat leaf parsley
18		whole shallots, peeled	2	Tbs	chopped coriander
4		garlic cloves, crushed	1		preserved lemon, rind of, minced
1	Tbs	all-purpose flour	4	oz	pitted medjool dates, chopped
			1	Tbs	clear honey

Procedure

1 Place the lamb in a bowl and add the ground coriander, ginger, saffron and olive oil.
2 Mix well and leave to marinate for 24 hours.
3 Brown off the lamb and set aside.
4 Fry the shallots until lightly golden then add the garlic and the lamb.
5 Add the flour, tomato puree and cinnamon stick.
6 Stir in the lamb stock and bring to the boil.
7 Cover tightly and simmer gently for 1 1/2 hours.
8 Add the parsley, coriander, lemon rind, dates and honey.
9 Accompaniments Serve with spiced couscous.
10 This sounds like the type of thing that might work well in a crockpot.

Servings: 6

Moroccan Chicken and Date Tagine Recipe

A taste of African cuisine...

* 1 large red onion, thinly sliced
* 1 unwaxed lemon, zested
* 4 fresh dates or soft dried dates
* 2 large boneless skinless chicken breasts
* 3 tablespoons olive oil
* 50 g pine nuts
* salt and pepper
* 1 teaspoon harissa
* 350 ml chicken stock
* 200 g couscous
* 1 tablespoon butter
* 1 tablespoon chopped coriander

Procedure

1 Cut the dates in half, discard the stone and then chop into six pieces.
2 Slice the chicken into short strips.
3 Heat two tablespoons of olive oil in a frying pan and stir in the onion.
4 Cook until slippery and soft, then add in the pine kernels and lemon zest, salt and pepper.
5 Turn down the heat and cook for about five minutes, before adding in the chicken.
6 Cook until the meat is lightly browned.
7 Squeeze the juice from half the lemon over the top, stir in the harissa, stock and dates.
8 Simmer for 10-15 minutes, stirring occasionally, until the water is reduced by half.
9 You should end up with a thick, rusty coloured sauce.
10   Meanwhile, prepare the couscous by placing it in a bowl and adding 300ml boiling water, remaining olive oil and salt.
11   Cover and leave for 15 minutes, then use a fork to loosen the grains and mix in the butter.
12   Serve the chicken mixture over the couscous, garnished with some chopped coriander and a lemon wedge.

Servings: 2

Preparation Time: 20 minutes
Cooking Time: 55 minutes

Moroccan Chicken Stew

A kdra is akin to the long-cooked North African clay-pot dish known as a tagine.

1 3		1/2-lb. chicken, cut into 8 pieces, skin removed	2 yellow onions, thinly sliced
1	cup	blanched whole almonds	4 cups chicken broth
		1/4 tsp. turmeric or saffron	1/4 cup chopped parsley
1	tsp	ground white pepper	Kosher salt, to taste
1	tsp	ground dried ginger	1/2 cup canned chickpeas, drained
1		cinnamon stick	2 Tbs fresh lemon juice
2	Tbs	smen (see note, below) or butter	

Procedure

1 Combine chicken, almonds, turmeric, pepper, ginger, cinnamon, and smen in a medium pot over medium heat; cook, turning, 3–4 minutes. Add half the onions and broth; boil. Reduce to medium-low; cook, covered, for 30 minutes.

2 Add remaining onion and parsley to chicken; cover and cook until chicken is very tender, 25–30 minutes. Remove chicken; set aside. Bring sauce to a boil; cook until thickened, 13–15 minutes. Return chicken to pot along with salt and chickpeas; heat through. Drizzle in lemon juice and serve.

Servings: 4

Author Notes

Note: To make smen, cut 16 tbsp. unsalted butter into chunks; knead in a bowl with 6 tbsp. fine sea salt. Form butter into 8 patties; stack in an earthenware container and cover; set aside to let rest in a cool, dark place for 2 weeks. Melt butter in a pot over low heat, without stirring, removing foam, until clear, 20–25 minutes. Cool. Strain through a cheesecloth-lined sieve.

Repeat. Discard solids; spoon into a jar. Seal; store in a cool, dark spot for a month. Makes about 1/4 cup.

Moroccan Chicken Tagine

2		frozen barbecued chickens with sauce -- defrosted	8	oz	shredded carrots
		--kosher precooked	2	tsp	garlic powder
8	oz	frozen chopped peppers & onions	2	Tbs	honey
1/2 cup		orange-flavored brandy	1/2 cup		lemon juice
8	oz	mixed dried fruits -- cut in half	2	cups	coarsely cut italian parsley
		--see note			sliced almonds
14	oz	stewed tomatoes -- partially drained	1		sprig italian parsley -- for garnish
2	tsp	five-spice powder			

Procedure

1 Drain barbecue sauce from defrosted chickens. Reserve. Cut each chicken into 8 pieces and place, skin side up, in a baking pan. Remove any fat from reserved sauce. Place 2 cups sauce in large microwave dish. Dispose of remaining sauce. Mix in peppers and onions, brandy, dried fruits, tomatoes, five-spice powder, carrots, garlic powder, honey, lemon juice and parsley. Partially cover and microwave on high 7 minutes, until fruits are fork-tender. Pour sauce and its contents over chicken and marinate overnight. Sprinkle with almonds and bake in preheated 350-degree oven for 45 minutes until heated completely through. Garnish with parsley before serving. This goes beautifully with a couscous mix, which cooks in 5 minutes, or barley pilaf, which microwaves in 8 minutes. Just follow the package directions.

Servings: 12

Moroccan Chicken Tagine with Couscous

This Moroccan chicken dish, named after the clay vessel in which it's traditionally cooked, is even better when garnished with caramelized onions, raisins and almonds.

1		chicken, about 3 pounds, cut into 8 pieces
		coarse salt and freshly ground black pepper to taste
3	Tbs	extra-virgin olive oil
1/2		onion, cut into 1/4-inch dice
2		cloves garlic, minced
1	tsp	ground cumin
1	tsp	curry powder
1	tsp	ground cinnamon
1	tsp	ground coriander
1	tsp	turmeric
		pinch of saffron threads
		juice of 1 lemon
1		bunch cilantrom stems discarded, roughly chopped
2	cups	chicken stock
2		medium zucchini, each cut into 8 slices
1		yellow squash, cut into 8 slices
2		medium carrots, each cut into 8 slices
2		medium turnips, each cut into 8 slices
		Couscous (recipe follows):
1 1/4	cups	water or chicken stock
1		6-ounce box Moroccan or other couscous
1	Tbs	olive oil
1	tsp	ground cumin
		coarse salt and freshly ground black pepper to taste

Procedure

1 Bring the water to a boil. Stir the remaining ingredients together in a bowl and cover with the boiling water. Cover

with plastic wrap and let sit until all the liquid is absorbed, about 15 minutes.

2 Season the chicken pieces with salt and pepper.

3 In a saucepot big enough to hold the chicken and the chicken stock, heat the olive oil over moderate heat. Add the onion, garlic, and spices to the pan and saute until the onion is soft, about 4-5 minutes.

4 Add the lemon juice, cilantro, chicken pieces, and chicken stock to the pan. Raise the heat to high and bring the stock to a boil.

5 Reduce the heat to a simmer, cover, and cook until the chicken is tender, about 45 minutes.

6 Remove the chicken from the pan and add the zucchini, squash, carrots and turnips. Cook until the vegetables are tender, about 10 minutes. Return the chicken to the pot.

7 To serve, mound equal portions of the couscous on each of 4 dinner plates. Spoon some chicken and vegetables on top of the couscous and spoon some of the sauce over and around the plate.

Servings: 4

Moroccan Chicken Tagine With Honey and Apricots

This is another one of those amazing recipes that I get from my upstairs neighbor. I have to actually watch her cook so I can get approximate measurements. In my next life, I want to be Moroccan!

* 6 lbs chicken pieces
* 1 large yellow onion
* 1 cup margarine (1 cup)
* 1/2 teaspoon turmeric
* salt
* 1 teaspoon black pepper
* 2 cinnamon sticks
* 1 lb dried apricot or prune
* 8 tablespoons honey
* 2 teaspoons ground cinnamon
* 1/2 cup peeled almonds
* 1 tablespoon sesame seed
* oil

Procedure

1 In a large pot, melt the margarine.
2 Fry the chopped onions until soft, then add the chicken, salt, pepper, turmeric and cinnamon sticks.
3 Don't worry, no one will make you eat a cinnamon stick unless you really want to.
4 Add enough water to cover the chicken, about two cups.
5 Bring to a boil, reduce the heat, and simmer until the chicken is done, adding water if necessary.
6 Remove the chicken pieces.
7 Add the apricots and simmer for about fifteen minutes.
8 Add the ground cinnamon and the honey, stir and cook until the sauce has a honey-like consistency.
9 Add more honey if necessary.
10   When the sauce is almost ready, saute the almonds in oil.
11   Drain most of the oil from the pan, and toast the sesame seeds.
12   Return the chicken to the pot and reheat.

13   Place the chicken on a serving tray, pour the sauce on top of it and top with the almonds and the sesame seeds.

14   Serve with couscous (except on Passover).

Servings: 6

Preparation Time: 15 minutes

Moroccan Lamb Tagine Smothered With Olives

1	pinch	ground saffron
1	tsp	ground ginger
1	tsp	freshly-ground black pepper
1/2 tsp		ground cumin
1	tsp	sweet paprika
1	Tbs	minced garlic
1	Tbs	salt
3	Tbs	olive oil
3	lbs	lamb shoulder, trimmed ,and cut into 2" pieces

1	cup	grated yellow onions, rinsed, and squeezed dry
		Freshly-ground black pepper, to taste
3	cups	dark veal or chicken stock
2/3 cup		finely-chopped fresh parsley, plus extra for garnish
1/3 cup		finely-chopped fresh cilantro
1	lb	cracked green olives, drained, pitted
3	Tbs	fresh lemon juice - (to 5)
		Pine Nut And Preserved Lemon Couscous, (see recipe)

Procedure

1 In the cup of a small food processor, combine the saffron, ginger, pepper, cumin, paprika, garlic, salt and 2 tablespoons of the oil. Process until smooth.

2 In a large mixing bowl, toss the shoulder with the above mixture. Mix well. Heat the remaining tablespoon of oil in large cast-iron or heavy bottom pot over medium heat. Add the lamb and sear for 2 to 3 minutes. Stir in the onions. Season with pepper. Cook for 2 minutes. Stir in the stock. Add the herbs and bring to a boil. Reduce the heat to low and simmer, uncovered until the meat is very tender, about 2 hours.

3 Using a slotted spoon, remove the meat from the pan and set aside. Remove any scum that has risen to the surface of the liquid. Add the olives to the cooking liquid, increase the heat to high and boil for about 10 minutes or until the mixture is like a thick gravy. Stir in the lemon juice and reseason if necessary.

4 About 30 minutes before serving, preheat the oven to 450 degrees. Place the meat in a shallow ovenproof serving dish and cook until the meat is lightly crisped, about 15 to 20 minutes. Serve the lamb with the Pine Nut And Preserved Lemon Couscous. Garnish with parsley.

Servings: 6

Moroccan Lamb Tagine with Raisins, Almonds, and Honey

2	tsp	ras-el-hanout*
2	tsp	salt
3/4	tsp	black pepper
3/4	tsp	ground ginger
1/4	tsp	crumbled saffron threads
3		cups water
3	lb	boneless lamb shoulder, cut into 1-inch cubes
1		large onion, coarsely grated (1 cup)
2		garlic cloves, finely chopped
2		(3-inch) cinnamon sticks
1/2		stick (1/4 cup) unsalted butter, cut into pieces
1 1/4		cups raisins
1 1/4		cups whole blanched almonds
1/2	cup	honey
1	tsp	ground cinnamon Accompaniment: couscous

Procedure

1 Whisk together ras-el-hanout, salt, pepper, ginger, saffron, and 1 cup water in a 5-quart heavy pot. Stir in lamb, remaining 2 cups water, onion, garlic, cinnamon sticks, and butter and simmer, covered, until lamb is just tender, about 1 1/2 hours.

2 Stir in raisins, almonds, honey, and ground cinnamon and simmer, covered, until meat is very tender, about 30 minutes more.

3 Uncover pot and cook over moderately high heat, stirring occasionally, until stew is slightly thickened, about 15 minutes more.

Servings: 4

Author Notes

Tagine can be made 1 day ahead and cooled, uncovered, then chilled, covered.

Moroccan Lamb Tagine with Raisins, Almonds, and Honey

* 2 teaspoons ras-el-hanout*
* 2 teaspoons salt
* 3/4 teaspoon black pepper
* 3/4 teaspoon ground ginger
* 1/4 teaspoon crumbled saffron threads
* 3 cups water
* 3 lb boneless lamb shoulder, cut into 1-inch cubes
* 1 large onion, coarsely grated (1 cup)
* 2 garlic cloves, finely chopped
* 2 (3-inch) cinnamon sticks
* 1/2 stick (1/4 cup) unsalted butter, cut into pieces
* 1 1/4 cups raisins
* 1 1/4 cups whole blanched almonds
* 1/2 cup honey
* 1 teaspoon ground cinnamon
* Accompaniment: couscous

Procedure

1 Whisk together ras-el-hanout, salt, pepper, ginger, saffron, and 1 cup water in a 5-quart heavy pot. Stir in lamb, remaining 2 cups water, onion, garlic, cinnamon sticks, and butter and simmer, covered, until lamb is just tender, about 1 1/2 hours.

2 Stir in raisins, almonds, honey, and ground cinnamon and simmer, covered, until meat is very tender, about 30 minutes more.

3 Uncover pot and cook over moderately high heat, stirring occasionally, until stew is slightly thickened, about 15 minutes more.

Servings: 6

Total Time: 180 minutes

Author Notes

Cooks' note: •Tagine can be made 1 day ahead and cooled, uncovered, then chilled, covered.

Moroccan Pork Tagine

Tagine is a traditional Moroccan stew typically made with chicken or lamb, vegetables and spices that is served over couscous. This tagine features pork tenderloin, which is naturally very lean and flavorful.

1	lb	454g / 16oz Well-trimmed pork tenderloin - cut 3/4" medallions	1	Tbs	15ml Olive oil
			1	Tbs	15ml Onion - chopped (medium)
1	Tbs	15ml All-purpose flour	3		Garlic cloves - minced
1	tsp	5ml Ground cumin	2 1/2	cups	592ml Canned chicken broth - divided
1	tsp	5ml Paprika			
1/4	tsp	1.3ml Powdered saffron = (or 1/2 tspn turmeric)	1/3	cup	53g / 1.9oz Golden or dark raisins
			1	cup	237ml Quick-cooking couscous
1/4	tsp	1.3ml Freshly-ground ground red pepper	1/4	cup	4g / 0.1oz Chopped fresh cilantro
1/4	tsp	1.3ml Ground ginger	1/4	cup	23g / 0.8oz Sliced toasted almonds - (optional)

Procedure

1 Toss pork with flour, cumin, paprika, saffron, pepper and ginger in medium bowl; set aside.

2 Heat oil in large nonstick skillet over medium-high heat. Add onion; cook 5 minutes, stirring occasionally. Add pork and garlic; cook 4 to 5 minutes or until pork is no longer pink, stirring occasionally.

3 Add 3/4 cup chicken broth and raisins; bring to a boil over high heat. Reduce heat to medium; simmer, uncovered, 7 to 8 minutes or until pork is cooked through, stirring occasionally.

4 Meanwhile, bring remaining 1 3/4 cups chicken broth to a boil in medium saucepan. Stir in couscous. Cover; remove from heat. Let stand 5 minutes or until liquid is absorbed.

5 Spoon couscous onto 4 plates; top with pork mixture. Sprinkle with cilantro and almonds, if desired.

Servings: 4

Moroccan Pork Tagine

1	lb	well-trimmed pork tenderloin, cut 3/4" medallions	1	Tbs	olive oil
			1		medium onion, chopped
1	Tbs	all-purpose flour	3		garlic cloves, minced
1	tsp	ground cumin			
1	tsp	paprika	2 1/2	cups	canned chicken broth, divided
1/4	tsp	powdered saffron = (or 1/2 tspn turmeric)	1/3	cup	golden or dark raisins
1/4	tsp	freshly-ground ground red pepper	1	cup	quick-cooking couscous
1/4	tsp	ground ginger	1/4	cup	chopped fresh cilantro
			1/4	cup	sliced toasted almonds, (optional)

Procedure

1 Toss pork with flour, cumin, paprika, saffron, pepper and ginger in medium bowl; set aside.

2 Heat oil in large nonstick skillet over medium-high heat. Add onion; cook 5 minutes, stirring occasionally. Add pork and garlic; cook 4 to 5 minutes or until pork is no longer pink, stirring occasionally.

3 Add 3/4 cup chicken broth and raisins; bring to a boil over high heat. Reduce heat to medium; simmer, uncovered, 7 to 8 minutes or until pork is cooked through, stirring occasionally.

4 Meanwhile, bring remaining 1 3/4 cups chicken broth to a boil in medium saucepan. Stir in couscous. Cover; remove from heat. Let stand 5 minutes or until liquid is absorbed.

5 Spoon couscous onto 4 plates; top with pork mixture. Sprinkle with cilantro and almonds, if desired.

Servings: 4

Author Notes

Tagine is a traditional Moroccan stew typically made with chicken or lamb, vegetables and spices that is served over couscous. This tagine features pork tenderloin, which is naturally very lean and flavorful.

Moroccan Spiced Meatballs W/ Eggs in Tomato Sauce

Meatballs

1	lb	ground lamb or ground beef
1/2		onion, grated
1/2 tsp		salt
1/4 tsp		pepper
1/2 tsp		sweet Hungarian paprika
2		sprigs fresh coriander, finely chopped
2		sprigs flat leaf parsley, finely chopped

Sauce

2	Tbs	olive oil
1/2		onion, grated
1/2 tsp		salt
1/2 tsp		sweet Hungarian paprika
1/8 tsp		ground ginger
1/4 tsp		turmeric
1/2 tsp		cayenne pepper
3	Tbs	tomato paste
1	cup	lamb stock or beef stock

Vegetables and Eggs

2	cups	squash or potatoes, peeled & cut into large chunks
1/2 cup		peas
3		eggs, beaten

Procedure

1 Use your hands to mix the meatball ingredients, and roll mixture into mini meatballs 3/4"-1" in diameter; set aside.
2 In a skillet or tajine combine sauce ingredients and let mixture simmer, covered, over low heat for 5 minutes.
3 Add meatballs, squash, and peas to the suace and simmer, covered, over medium-low heat for 15 minutes.
4 Pour the eggs in in a stream over everything.
5 Cover and cook just long enough to cook the egg (about 3 minutes, depending on how well done you like your eggs).
6 Serve warm over couscous, sprinkled with cumin or black pepper if desired.

Servings: 4

Moroccan Tagine

"An exotic warm stew that is loved by all and is very easy to make. Also delicious as a vegetarian dish, without chicken. Serve over couscous."

15	ml	olive oil
2		skinless, boneless chicken breast halves - cut into chunks
0.5		onion, chopped
3		cloves garlic, minced
1		small butternut squash, peeled and chopped
440.2 g		garbanzo beans, drained and rinsed
15	ml	olive oil
2		skinless, boneless chicken breast halves - cut into chunks
0.5		onion, chopped
3		cloves garlic, minced
1		small butternut squash, peeled and chopped
440.2 g		garbanzo beans, drained and rinsed
1		carrot, peeled and chopped
1		(14.5 ounce) can diced tomatoes with juice
1		(14 ounce) can vegetable broth
10	g	sugar
15	ml	lemon juice
6	g	salt
2	g	ground coriander
1	dash	cayenne pepper

Procedure

1 Heat the olive oil in a large skillet over medium heat, and cook the chicken, onion, and garlic about 15 minutes, until browned.

2 Mix the squash, garbanzo beans, carrot, tomatoes with juice, broth, sugar, and lemon juice into the skillet. Season with salt, coriander, and cayenne pepper. Bring the mixture to a boil, and continue cooking 30 minutes, until vegetables are tender.

Servings: 6

Preparation Time: 15 minutes

Cooking Time: 45 minutes
Total Time: 60 minutes

Moroccan tagine

FOR THE CHERMOULA PASTE

2	red onions , chopped
3	garlic cloves
	small knob fresh root ginger, peeled
	100ml/3 ½ fl oz lemon juice (about 3 lemons)
	100ml/3 ½ fl oz olive oil
1 Tbs	each honey, cumin, paprika, turmeric
1 tsp	hot chilli powder
	handful coriander , chopped

FOR THE TAGINE

1 Tbs	olive oil
3	carrots , cut into chunks
3	large parsnips , cut into chunks
3	red onions , cut into chunks
2	large potatoes , cut into chunks
4	leeks , ends trimmed and cut into chunks
12	dried prunes , dates or figs
2	sprigs mint , leaves only, finely chopped

Procedure

1 To make the chermoula, whizz paste ingredients in a blender. Heat oven to 220C/fan 200C/gas 7. Tip the oil and vegetables into a heatproof casserole and cook on the hob until lightly browned, about 7 mins. You may have to do this in two batches

2 Add the chermoula paste to the casserole, along with the dried fruit. Pour in 400ml water, cover with a lid and cook in the oven for 45 mins. Reduce heat to 180C/fan 160C/gas 4 and cook for another 45 mins. Sprinkle with the mint. Serve on its own or with couscous or crusty bread.

Servings: 6

Moroccan Tagine

"Tagines are Moroccan slow-cooked meat, fruit and vegetable dishes which are almost invariably made with mutton. Using lamb cuts down the cooking time, but if you can find good hogget (older than lamb, younger than mutton, commonly labeled 'baking legs' and sold cheaply) that will do very well."

15	ml	olive oil
2		large onions, peeled and sliced into rings
905	g	lamb meat, cut into 1 1/2 inch cubes
2	g	ground cumin
2	g	ground coriander seed
2	g	ground ginger
2	g	ground cinnamon

		salt to taste
2	g	ground black pepper
4		pears - peeled, cored and cut into 1 1/2 inch chunks
80	g	golden raisins
70	g	blanched slivered almonds

Procedure

1 Heat the oil in a large pot or Dutch oven over medium heat. Fry the onion in the oil until soft. Add the lamb meat to the pan, and fry until just browned on the outside. Season with cumin, coriander, ginger, cinnamon, salt and pepper. Pour just enough water into the pot to cover the meat. Cover, and simmer over low heat for 1 1/2 to 2 hours, until meat is tender and the mixture is stew-like. Displace lid a little after an hour if there appears to be too much liquid.

2 Add the pears, golden raisins and almonds to the stew, and cook for another 5 minutes or so, until the pears are soft. Serve with rice.

Servings: 5

Total Time: 135 minutes

Moroccan Tagine - Chicken or Quorn

I make this with Quorn pieces instead of chicken and it's really tasty, so it's probably amazing with chicken. Serve with cous cous. This recipe is enough for two really greedy people.

Slosh of olive oil for frying.

1 onion

2 cloves of garlic, roughly chopped

chilli to taste eg. not overpowering or painful amounts

½ tsp ground cinnamon

1 tsp of mild curry powder

½ tsp tumeric

½ tsp cumin (or cumin seeds if you like)

½ packet of Quorn pieces (for 2 people) or 250-ish grams diced chicken breast

1 courgette cut into nice chunks

1 leek sliced into thick rings

Around 500 ml of vegetable stock or chicken stock- Marigold Swiss Vegetable Bouillon stock is what I use, it might even be vegan, and it is totally brilliant and everyone should have some. Also you don't need to use

3 bay leaves

1 tsp thyme.

6 cherry tomatoes

A handful of dried apricots roughly chopped- I really like a brand called Crazy Jacks 'cos they are sulphite free and really dark and moist, but I've only seen them in Sainsbury's.

You're supposed to add some lemon juice before you serve it but I always forget.

And some mint leaves, but I don't own any.

salt if you're using this.

Procedure

1 Frying: start with the onions, add the leek and courgette, garlic, then quorn chunks then chilli and spices until your housemates start saying "wow, that smells amazing" (10 mins approx)

2 Add stock, bay leaves, thyme and apricots and bring to a vigorous bubble. Add the tomatoes, turn down to a simmer and cook for half an hour or until the veg are at your preferred texture and the tomatoes have burst. The liquids need to reduce a bit, so don't cover the pan.

3 Add lemon juice and mint leaves if you can be bothered. Serve with cous cous.

Chicken version (I've never done this one)

4 Fry onion, chilli, garlic and spices for 5 minutes

5 Add the chicken, courgette and leeks and fry for another 5 minutes.

6 Pour in chicken stock, bay leaves, thyme and apricots. Bring to a bubble, add the tomatoes, turn down and simmer for half an hour.

Servings: 2

Moroccan-Spiced Chicken Tagine

If you can't find a package of thighs at the market, buy whole chickens. You (or the butcher) can cut up the chickens and freeze the leftover pieces for another use.

3/4	lb	340g / 11oz Boneless skinless chicken thighs - cut 1/2" strips
1/2	tsp	2.5ml Salt
2	Tbs	30ml Olive oil
1/2	cup	31g / 1.1oz Chopped red onion
1	cup	237ml Zucchini - shredded (medium)
1/3	cup	20g / 0.7oz Chopped drained sun-dried tomatoes
2 1/2	cups	592ml Chicken broth
1		Garbanzo beans - (15 1/2 oz) - rinsed, drained
3	Tbs	45ml Golden raisins
1 1/2	tsp	7.5ml Ground cumin
1	tsp	5ml Crumbled saffron threads
1/2	tsp	2.5ml Ground allspice
1/2	tsp	2.5ml Ground nutmeg
1/4	tsp	1.3ml Freshly-ground white pepper
1	cup	237ml Uncooked couscous
3	Tbs	45ml Chopped fresh cilantro leaves - for garnish

Servings: 6

Moroccan-Spiced Chicken Tagine

* 3/4 pound boneless, skinless chicken thighs, cut into 1/2-inch strips
* 1/2 teaspoon salt
* 2 tablespoons olive oil
* 1/2 cup chopped red onion
* 1 medium-sized zucchini, shredded
* 1/3 cup drained and chopped sun-dried tomatoes
* 2 1/2 cups chicken broth
* 1 can (15 1/2 ounces) garbanzo beans, rinsed and drained
* 3 tablespoons golden raisins
* 1 1/2 teaspoons ground cumin
* 1 teaspoon crumbled saffron threads
* 1/2 teaspoon ground allspice
* 1/2 teaspoon ground nutmeg
* 1/4 teaspoon ground white pepper
* 1 cup uncooked couscous
* 3 tablespoons chopped fresh cilantro leaves, for garnish

Procedure

1 Sprinkle the chicken with salt. Place the olive oil in a large Dutch oven over medium heat. Add the chicken, onion, zucchini and tomatoes. Cook, stirring, until the chicken is no longer pink and the vegetables are tender, about 4 to 6 minutes.

2 Add all remaining ingredients except the couscous and cilantro. Bring to a boil over high heat. Stir in the couscous, cover, and remove from the heat. Let stand for 5 to 7 minutes or until the liquid is absorbed. Fluff the couscous with a fork. Serve sprinkled with cilantro.

Servings: 4

Preserved Lemons

Preserved lemons are a staple in Moroccan cuisine and are frequently used in stews or tagines. Although easy to prepare, this step must be done well in advance, since curing the lemons takes at least one month.

4   lemons, depending on size
    1/4-cup coarse salt, more
    if desired (kosher or coarse
    sea salt)
6   coriander seeds

6   black peppercorns
1   cinnamon stick
4   whole cloves
    Lemon juice

Procedure

1 Make two cuts in lemon, from the top to within 1/2 inch of the bottom, nearly quartering them. Sprinkle salt on inside surface before reshaping.

2 Place 1 tablespoon salt on the bottom of a 1 -1/2 pint size jar. Place lemons in jar and push them down, adding more salt, and spices in between. Press the lemons into jar and add fresh lemon juice to approximately 3/4" from top of jar.

3 Allow lemons to ripen in a warm place. Invert jar upside daily (if possible). Takes approximately 30 days. May keep up to one year.

Servings: 4

Quince And Okra Tagine With Moha

Procedure

1 Coarse salt, to taste

2 Juice of 4 lemons

3 large quartered quinces, seeded

4 chicken - (abt 4 lbs) skinned, and

5 cut into 8 pieces

6 cups   water - (to 5)

7 /2 Tbs   olive oil

8 large onion, sliced

9 tsp   minced garlic

10   tsp   ground cumin

11   tsp   ground ginger

12   tsp   saffron threads

13   Freshly-ground black pepper, to taste

14   lb   fresh okra, stems trimmed

15   Cooked couscous, for serving

16   Prepare an ice-water bath. Bring a large saucepan of salted water to a boil. Add quinces and juice of two lemons. Cook for 5 minutes. Transfer the quinces to the ice-water bath. Drain, and set aside.

17   In a large bowl, combine chicken, 4 cups water, the remaining juice of 2 lemons, and 1 teaspoon salt. Let stand for 15 minutes.

18   In a medium saucepan, heat 2 tablespoons olive oil. Add half the onion, and cook until translucent, about 5 minutes. Remove from heat, and set aside.

19   Place a flame tamer over burner. Heat remaining 5 1/2 tablespoons olive oil in a medium tagine or saucepan set on flame tamer over low heat. Add remaining onion, garlic, cumin, ginger, and saffron. Season with salt and pepper. Cook until onions have softened, about 5 minutes.

20   Drain chicken, and add to tagine. Cook chicken, covered, stirring until well coated with the spice mixture, about 5 minutes.

21   Arrange okra evenly over chicken. Top with blanched quinces and 1/4 cup water. Cook, covered, adding more water if necessary, until chicken is cooked through, about 30 minutes.

22   Top with reserved onions, and serve immediately.

Servings: 4

Author Notes

Comments: Tagines are savory Moroccan stews commonly served with couscous, and traditionally combine a meat with vegetables, fruit, or both, as in this recipe. Although the name refers to the vessel in which tagines are conventionally cooked, this version may be prepared in a medium saucepan.

Slow Cooker Root Vegetable Tagine

"This is a subtly spiced, super easy slow cooker meal. A good introduction to Moroccan food. Serve with couscous."

455 g	parsnips, peeled and diced	2	g	ground cumin
455 g	turnips, peeled and diced	0.9 g		ground ginger
220 g	onions, chopped	1	g	ground cinnamon
455 g	carrots, peeled and diced	0.4 g		ground cayenne pepper
6	dried apricots, chopped	1	g	dried parsley
4	pitted prunes, chopped	2	g	dried cilantro
2	g ground turmeric	1		(14 ounce) can vegetable broth

Procedure

1 In a slow cooker, toss together the parsnips, turnips, onions, carrots, apricots, and prunes. Season with turmeric, cumin, ginger, cinnamon, cayenne pepper, parsley, and cilantro. Pour in the vegetable broth.

2 Cover, and cook 9 hours on Low.

Servings: 6

Preparation Time: 50 minutes
Cooking Time: 540 minutes

Smen

Smen is a type of preserved clarified butter prepared in a way similar to Indian ghee. It may be flavored with wild herbs. It has quite a potent cheese taste that takes a little getting used to, especially for eating on bread. In cooking, smen lends a characteristic flavor to tagines, k'dras and couscous. In some Fez and Berber households, smen is packed in glass jars and kept for years, gradually becoming darker and more pungent with time.

2 cups sweet butter, diced   1/4 tsp herbes de Provence
1 Tbs coarse salt

Procedure

1 Gently heat the butter in a saucepan until melted, then bring to the

2 boil. Lower the heat and simmer for 3-4 minutes until the butter is clear and

3 there is a separate layer on the bottom of the pan. Line a sieve with muslin

4 that has been wrung out in hot water, and sprinkle with the salt and herb.

5 Gradually spoon the clear butter into the sieve and allow it to strain

6 through. Then strain it again into a clean, dry jar. Cover and keep in the

7 refrigerator for up to 6 weeks.

Servings: 1

Spiced Chicken Apricot Tajine

8	broiler-fryer chicken thighs, skinned	2	sticks (3 inches each) cinnamon
1/4 cup	honey		Juice of 1 lemon
1	large onion, chopped	2 tsp	tumeric
3	cloves garlic, minced	1/2 cup	dried apricot quarters

Procedure

1 Arrange broiler-fryer chicken thighs in bottom of Dutch oven.

2 Pour honey over chicken; sprinkle with onion and then with minced garlic. Add cinnamon sticks and sprinkle with lemon juice and tumeric. Top with apricot quarters, cover.

3 Bake in 350 degrees F. oven for about 2 hours or until fork can be inserted in chicken with ease.

4 Remove cinnamon sticks from chicken mixture and serve with rice.

Servings: 4

Spicy Lamb Tagine with Couscous

Very, very good Moroccan stew over fluffy couscous.Delicious for dinner tonight!!Wonderfull change!

* 1 3/4 lbs lean lamb leg steak
* 1 1/2 ounces onions, chopped
* 2 cloves garlic, chopped
* 1/2 teaspoon cayenne pepper
* 2 inches cinnamon sticks, broken in half
* 1 teaspoon ground ginger
* 1 teaspoon paprika
* 10-12 saffron strands
* turmeric, if you want a little colour
* salt and pepper
* 4 1/2 ounces ready to eat dried apricots, quartered
* 6 ounces carrots, diced
* 3 1/2 ounces zucchini, diced
* 12 ounces tomatoes, chopped
* 2 tablespoons chopped fresh coriander (chopped)
* 2 tablespoons chopped fresh parsley
* 10 ounces couscous

garnish
* fresh coriander
* parsley

Procedure

1 Trim any fat off the lamb and cut it into 1 inch cubes.

2 Put the meat, onions, garlic, cayenne pepper, cinnamon, ginger, paprika and saffron if using,into the bottom of a double boiler or a large saucepan, season to taste and add enough water to cover.

3 Bring the contents to a boil, then cover the pan, reduce the heat to low, and simmer for 1 hour 30 minutes.

4 Add the apricots, carrots,zucchini,tomatoes, coriander and parsley to the pan and cook, covered for a further 15 minutes.

5 Meanwhile, following package directions, prepare enough couscous for 6 people.

6 Add salt to taste.

7 To serve, spoon the couscous onto serving dish, lift the lamb and vegetables from the pan with a slotted spoon and lay

them on top of the couscous and sprinkle them with chopped coriander and parsley.

8 Pour the broth into a jug or bowl to serve separately and let people help themselves at the table.

Servings: 6

Preparation Time: 15 minutes
Cooking Time: 120 minutes

Spicy Potato Tagine with Preserved Lemon and Olives

* 2 pounds red potatoes
* 1 small onion, grated and squeezed dry (see Note), plus 1 medium onion, thinly sliced
* 3 tablespoons extra virgin olive oil
* 1/3 cup grated tomato (see Tips, below)
* 1/4 teaspoon ground ginger
* 1/4 teaspoon hot Hungarian paprika
* Pinch of ground cumin
* 1 teaspoon crushed garlic
* 1 bay leaf
* 1/4 fresh lemon
* 2 tablespoons chopped flat-leaf parsley
* 2 tablespoons chopped fresh cilantro
* Salt
* 4 to 5 dry saffron threads, crumbled
* 24 juicy purple or tan olives
* 1/2 preserved lemon

Procedure

1 Peel the potatoes and thickly slice into a bowl of cold water.

2 In heavy saucepan set over moderate heat, cook the grated onion in olive oil until melting, 3 to 4 minutes. Add the tomato, ginger, paprika, cumin, and garlic. Cook, stirring, for 2 more minutes.

3 Drain the potatoes and add to the pan with the thinly sliced onion, the bay leaf, and the fresh lemon quarter. Toss to coat the potatoes, onion, and lemon quarter with the parsley, cilantro, and salt to taste. Add the saffron and 1 1/2 cups hot water and bring to a boil. Reduce the heat to very low and simmer until the potatoes are tender, about 40 minutes.

4 Use a slotted spatula to transfer to a covered serving dish to keep warm. Discard the lemon. Add the olives to the liquid and boil until the pan juices are reduced to a thick sauce. Correct the seasoning, pour over the potatoes, and garnish with the preserved lemon.

Servings: 6

Author Notes

To grate tomatoes: Halve and gently squeeze to remove the seeds. Grate the tomato halves, cut side facing the coarsest side of a box grater or flat shredder. You will be left with just the tomato skin on your hand; discard.

It's recommended cooking this dish the way Moroccans traditionally do: in a clay pot such as a Mexican cazuela or Moroccan tagine. The porous clay absorbs liquid from the dish, then slowly releases steam as it heats, which results in a more flavorful, juicy dish. Moroccan tagines are available at www.tagines.com. A note of warning: Clay pots are sensitive to rapid temperature changes, which can cause cracking. Don't put anything hot in a cold tagine or anything cold in a hot tagine. Consider investing in a flame-tamer or heat-diffuser (a metal plate that's placed over the burner) to distribute heat evenly.

Sweet Potato Tagine

14 1/2	oz low-sodium fat-free chicken broth -- or vegetable broth	10	dried tomato halves -- coarsely chopped
1/2	oz dried porcini mushrooms -- coarsely chopped	2 Tbs	fresh sage leaves -- chopped
4	sweet potatoes -- about 2 pounds, -- peeled & cut into -- chunks	3	cloves garlic -- chopped
		1/2 tsp	salt
		2 Tbs	olive oil
		2 cups	cooked couscous -- Israeli or Moroccan

Procedure

1 Preheat oven to 350 degrees F. In oven-proof casserole, combine broth and mushrooms; bring to a boil over high heat. Reduce heat to medium and simmer 2 minutes.

2 Remove the casserole from heat and add sweet potatoes, dried tomatoes, sage, garlic, and salt. Cover and bake in the oven for 30 minutes, stirring once.

3 Add the olive oil to sweet-potato mixture; stir and bake, uncovered, for 15 minutes longer. Stir well and cool at least 5 minutes before serving, allowing liquid in mixture to thicken slightly. Serve over couscous.

Servings: 4

Author Notes

Sweet potatoes contain more than 4 times the recommended daily
allowance of beta-carotene (more than carrots!), which protects against cancer
and heart disease. The tuber also contains high levels of vitamins C and E,
which bolster the immune system. Other nutrient bonuses: plenty of vitamin A,

potassium, iron, B vitamins, and fiber. Despite their rich taste, these
potatoes are fat- and cholesterol-free; a medium sweet potato has only about
130 calories.

Tagine

	Meat, see * Note 1		Freshly-ground black pepper, to taste
1	medium onion, chopped		
1	medium onion, quartered		Raisins
	Olive oil, as needed		Green olives, pitted
1 cup	water		Green peppers, cut into wedges
	Salt, to taste		Vegetables, see * Note 2
			Zucchini, (optional)

Procedure

1 Properly done, a tagine requires its specialized pot, a deep clay dish with a cone-like chimney. I have managed it in a large covered earthenware pot, but it requires letting the vapors escape a little -- the stewing is not as intense as typical American crockpot stews.

2 Heat a thin layer of olive oil in the pot or dish. Brown the meat and chopped onion. Add a cup of water, salt and pepper to taste, and vegetables. Cook on very low heat 20 to 25 minutes. Add raisins, olives, peppers, onion quarters, and zucchini and cook until vegetables are tender.

Servings: 4

Author Notes

* Note 1: Your choice (or mix) of chicken, lamb, or beef, cut into chunks.

* Note: Variety of cut vegetables that take a long time to cook (e.g. carrots, potatoes, beans, and/or turnips).

Spring-summer of 1975 found me in a town called Beni Mellal on the flank of the Atlas Mountains in Morocco, about equidistant from Fez and Marakech. I lived in a large but bare apartment on the second floor above a bordello, on a street known locally as La Rue d'Amour (the Street of Love) because so many bordellos were doing business on that block. Occasionally the police would raid, but not for sex. Located in a strict Muslim section of Morocco, they were on the prowl for alcoholic beverages.

The Madam, my landlady, was always tipped in advance that a raid was scheduled that night. As a foreigner, I was exempt from the Muslim rule, so she would carry her supply of beer and other alcoholic beverages up to my apartment and I would stash them in my closet for her until the raid had come and gone. In exchange, she would bring me huge platters of food. Among them was Tagine, a delicious stew.

I asked her how it was made, and she showed me. I have had tagines since at friends' homes in Morocco and in American restaurants, but never like the tagines she made me. Perhaps it was the sweet taste of having outwitted the morality police. Here is how I remember it.

Tagine Berber

We first tried this traditional Berber specialty in a tent at the Auberge Telouet, a restaurant in that Berber outpost in the High Atlas Mountains—and later developed this recipe at home. It is almost identical to the roadside version.

4	Tbs	olive oil
2	lbs	boneless lamb shoulder, cubed
2		medium onions, peeled and quartered
2	tsp	ground cumin
1/2	tsp	ground cinnamon
2	tsp	sweet paprika
	pinch	saffron threads
		Salt and freshly ground black pepper

2	medium Yukon gold potatoes, peeled and quartered
1	large carrot, peeled, halved crosswise, and quartered
1	large zucchini, halved crosswise and quartered
2	small white turnips, peeled and quartered
1	medium green pepper, trimmed and cut lengthwise into 1" strips
1	medium tomato, thinly sliced

Procedure

1 Heat 2 tbsp. oil in a large heavy-bottomed pot or tagine (a Moroccan cooking vessel) over high heat. Add lamb in batches and brown on all sides, stirring frequently. Set aside. In same pot, heat remaining 2 tbsp. oil over medium-low heat, add onions, cook for 15 minutes, then add cumin, cinnamon, paprika, and saffron and season to taste with salt and pepper. Stir, mixing well, and cook until onions are translucent, about 5 minutes more.

2 Return meat to pot and mix well. Form mixture into a mound in center of pot. Arrange potato quarters around meat, pressing angled sides into mound. Arrange carrots and zucchini the same way. Arrange turnip quarters and green pepper strips alternately around mound. Season vegetables with salt and pepper. Cook, covered, over medium-low heat, basting occasionally with liquid from bottom of pot, until

vegetables are cooked, about 1 1/4 hours. Arrange tomatoes atop meat, cook, covered, for 5 minutes more, and serve.

Servings: 6

Tagine of Chick Peas with Aromatics

4 cup	Chick peas, soaked	1/4 tsp	Hot red pepper
	Salt	1/4 tsp	Sweet red pepper
1	Spanish onion, grated	1/4 tsp	Cinnamon
3	lg Tomatoes, skinned, seeded &	1/4 tsp	Saffron
	-- diced	1/4 tsp	Cumin
6	Sprigs Italian parsley,	1/4 tsp	Ginger
	-- chopped		Black pepper
4	Sprigs cilantro, chopped	6 Tbs	Olive oil

Procedure

1 Drain chick peas & cook in boiling salted water until   tender. Drain. Peel chick peas & combine with onion   in a tagine (or shallow casserole).

2 Add tomatoes, herbs, spices, salt & pepper. Mix well.

3 When ready to cook, add olive oil & simmer over a low heat for 15 minutes or until the chick peas are well impregnated with the aromatoc flavours.

Servings: 4

Tagine of Lamb with Quinces

One of my favourite combinations-meat and fruit. You can use dates instead of prunes, and pears instead of quinces.

* 1 kg lamb shoulder, cut in 2 cm cubes
* 2 large onions, cut into 2 cm cubes
* 1/2 teaspoon mildly hot paprika
* 1 bunch fresh coriander, finely chopped
* 1/4 teaspoon powdered saffron
* 1/2 teaspoon ground ginger
* 500 g quinces, peeled,halved and cored
* 60 g butter
* 1 cup pitted prune

Procedure

1 Wash, top & tail the okra. String together with thread into a "necklace". Over high heat, cook the tomatoes with the parsley, paprika, garlic, salt & oil, mashing down the tomatoes as they cook. After 10 minutes, lower the heat to medium, add the okra & begin to poach iti n the sauce. From time to time lift up the necklace to stir. After the okra is tender, remove & keep warm. Continue to reduce the tomatoes until all the water has evaporated & the oil is released. Fry the tomatoes in this released oil, stirring continuously. Gently pull out the thread, place the okra in the serving dish. Pour the sauce over the top. Serve hot or lukewarm.

Servings: 6

Preparation Time: 40 minutes
Cooking Time: 120 minutes

Tagine of Okra and Tomatoes

1/2	lb	Okra	1 1/2	tsp	Sweet paprika
4 1/2	lb	Tomatoes, peeled, seeded & -- chopped	1	tsp	Garlic, chopped
					Salt
2	Tbs	Parsley, chopped	3	Tbs	Vegetable oil

Procedure

1 Wash, top & tail the okra. String together with thread into a "necklace". Over high heat, cook the tomatoes with the parsley, paprika, garlic, salt & oil, mashing down the tomatoes as they cook. After 10 minutes, lower the heat to medium, add the okra & begin to poach iti n the sauce. From time to time lift up the necklace to stir. After the okra is tender, remove & keep warm. Continue to reduce the tomatoes until all the water has evaporated & the oil is released. Fry the tomatoes in this released oil, stirring continuously. Gently pull out the thread, place the okra in the serving dish. Pour the sauce over the top. Serve hot or lukewarm.

Servings: 5

Tagine of pumpkin and chickpeas

This dish is beautifully rich and aromatic - a little sweet from the pumpkin and golden orange in colour. Perfect for a vegetarian dinner party.

1	cup	chickpeas, soaked overnight
2	Tbs	olive oil
1	Tbs	butter
1		large onion, chopped
2		cloves garlic, sliced
2	tsp	ground cumin
2	tsp	ground coriander
1		cinnamon stick
1/4 tsp		dried chilli flakes

1/4	tsp	saffron threads, steeped in 100ml hot water
		500g pumpkin, peeled and cut into large pieces
2		waxy potatoes, peeled and cut in half
half		a 400g tin tomatoes
2		zucchini, sliced
1/2		a preserved lemon, chopped
		cooked cous cous or rice, to serve
1/2	cup	yoghurt
1/2	cup	coriander leaves

Procedure

1 Put the chickpeas in a pot with plenty of cold water and boil for 30 minutes. Drain.

2 In a large pot, heat the oil and butter and cook the onion and garlic until soft and lightly golden.

3 Add the spices (except saffron), cook for a couple of minutes, then add the partially cooked chickpeas, saffron, pumpkin, potatoes, tomatoes and just enough water to cover. Season with salt and simmer gently until the potatoes are almost soft (about 30-40 minutes).

4 Add the zucchini and preserved lemon and cook for 5 more

5 minutes or until the potatoes and pumpkin are soft (but not mushy).

To serve

6 Serve with cous cous or rice and a dollop of yoghurt and some freshly chopped coriander.

Servings: 4

Author Notes

If you like it hot, serve a little harissa on the side (available at delis and some supermarkets).

Tagine of Spring Vegetables with Spiced Tomato Broth and Couscous

* 2 cups vegetable broth
* 2 cloves garlic, peeled
* 2 thin slices fresh ginger
* 1 tsp coriander
* 1 tsp cumin
* 1 small eggplant (or 2 Japanese eggplants), cut into 1/2-inch slices
* 1 tbsp tomato paste
* 1 cup baby carrots
* 1 cup cauliflower florets
* 1 medium zucchini, cut into 1/2-inch slices
* 1/2 cup sliced radishes
* 1 cup oyster mushrooms, bottom ends of stems trimmed (or button mushrooms, quartered)
* 1 cup frozen pearl onions
* 1 cup cherry tomatoes
* 2 cloves garlic, peeled and minced
* 2 tbsp extra-virgin olive oil
* 1 tbsp garam masala spice (found in supermarkets)
* 2 cups roughly chopped mustard greens
* 3 cups cooked whole-wheat couscous

Procedure

1 Preheat oven to 400°F. In a saucepan, simmer first 5 ingredients 20 minutes. Meanwhile, sprinkle eggplant with salt and let stand 10 minutes. Rinse and pat dry with a paper towel. Remove garlic cloves and ginger from saucepan. Add tomato paste and stir. Season with salt and pepper. Reserve and keep warm. Blanch carrots and cauliflower in boiling water 5 minutes; drain. Rinse with cold water; drain again. Toss all veggies, except mustard greens, with minced garlic and oil. Spread vegetables on baking sheet, sprinkle with garam masala and bake 15 minutes. Remove from oven, add mustard greens and toss. Return to oven and bake 5 minutes more. Divide couscous and vegetables among 4 bowls, and pour 1/2 cup broth in each.

Servings: 4

Tagine with Chicken

1		chicken filet (cubed)	2 Tbs	raisins
		Juice of 1/2 a lemon	1/2	an apple (cubed)
1 Tbs	curry paste		2	slices pineapple (cubed)
1 tsp	turmeric			
2 Tbs	parsley (finely chopped)			Salt and mild paprika
1	onion (chopped)			Olive oil

Procedure

1 Bake the chicken cubes in some olive oil in a pan to a golden brown. Season with salt and paprika. Put all the ingredients and the baked chicken cubes in the tagine. Add 20 cl water and bring to a boil. Put the lid on the tagine and let it simmer for 20 minutes on a low heat. Very tasty with some noodles.

Servings: 2

Tagine with Mince and Tomato

- 250 g (8 3/4oz) mince (lamb or your choice)
- pepper and salt
- 1/2 tsp cumin
- 1 tbsp of fresh coriander (finely chopped)
- 1 onion (finely chopped)
- 2 cloves of garlic (finely chopped)
- 1 cm of ginger (pressed)
- 500 g (1lb 2 1/2oz) tin of cubed tomatoes (or fresh)
- 1 tbsp of olive oil
- 1 egg
- 1 tsp of Ras El Hanout
- 2 tbsp of parsley (finely chopped)
- 1 handful of deepfreeze peas
- 1 tsp of Turmeric

Procedure

1 Season the mince with the pepper, salt, cumin, ras el hanout and parsley. Shape into small meatballs and fry them nice and brown. Put the rest of the ingredients into the tagine except for the egg and meatballs. Bring to the boil and allow it to simmer for 30 minutes. Add the meatballs and the egg and simmer for a further 10 minutes without the lid. You can add the meatballs from the beginning without frying them, but we think they are tastier fried. If you don't have a tagine you can make this dish in a stewing pan.

Servings: 2

Vegetable Tagine

1/4 cup	olive oil		2 Tbs	currants
1	large red pepper, chopped		1 tsp	ground cinnamon
			1	yellow squash, chopped
1	Tbs minced garlic		1	zucchini, chopped
1	Tbs minced shallots		2	ripe bananas
	Coarse salt		1 tsp	sugar
	Freshly ground pepper			
1	medium peeled eggplant, chopped			

Procedure

1 Heat 1 tablespoon olive oil in a large skillet over medium-high heat. Add red pepper and cook for 1 minute. Add 1 teaspoon garlic, 1 teaspoon shallots, and 1 tablespoon water. Cook until tender, about 3 minutes, stirring occasionally. Remove from pan and set aside.

2 Add 1 tablespoon olive oil to skillet and heat over medium-high heat. Add eggplant and season with salt and pepper. Cook for 1 minute, and add 1 teaspoon garlic, 1 teaspoon shallots, currants, and 1/2 teaspoon cinnamon. Cook until tender, stirring occasionally, about 3 to 4 minutes. Remove from pan and set aside.

3 Add 1 tablespoon olive oil to skillet and heat over medium-high heat. Add yellow squash and zucchini. Season with salt and pepper and add 1 teaspoon garlic and 1 teaspoon shallots. Cook until tender, but not falling apart, about 2 to 3 minutes. Remove from pan and set aside.

4 Heat oven to 375 degrees. Slice bananas crosswise and then lengthwise. Add 1 tablespoon olive oil to skillet and heat over medium-high heat. Add bananas, 1/2 teaspoon cinnamon, and sugar. Sauté until just soft, about 1 minute. Remove from pan and chop.

5 Combine all vegetables in a tagine or baking dish. Cover and transfer to oven and bake for 20 minutes.

Servings: 6

Vegetable Tagine

Though the word tagine refers to the cone-shaped cooking vessel that the dish is traditionally made in, it has also come to refer to Moroccan-style stew preparations. This version contains an assortment of vegetables, including cauliflower and chickpeas, making for a flavorful, filling vegetarian dish. What to buy: For a slacker solution, you can substitute high-quality canned chickpeas for the cooked chickpeas. Preserved lemons are a popular ingredient in Moroccan cooking. They're preserved in a salt-and-lemon-juice mixture and sold in jars. Look for them in gourmet grocery stores or online at igourmet.com.

For the tagine:

6 Tbs	olive oil
1	medium yellow onion, thinly sliced
2 tsp	ground cumin seed
1	cinnamon stick
1 tsp	grated fresh ginger
3	medium cloves garlic, thinly sliced
3	medium carrots, peeled, medium dice
1 cup	canned diced tomatoes in juice
1 quart	(4 cups) vegetable broth
pinch	saffron threads
1	medium head cauliflower, large dice
1 1/4 cup	green olives, such as picholine, pitted and halved
2 cups	cooked chickpeas, drained
1	preserved lemon, seeds removed, finely chopped
1/2 cup	dried currants

To serve:

3 cups	dry couscous
3 cups	water
1/2 cup	olive oil
1 cup	whole almonds, toasted
1/2 cup	sliced scallions
1/2 cup	plain Greek-style or whole-milk yogurt

Procedure

For the tagine:

1 Heat olive oil in a large Dutch oven or heavy-bottomed pot with a tightfitting lid over medium heat. When oil shimmers,

add onion, season with salt and freshly ground black pepper, and cook, stirring occasionally, until soft and translucent, about 5 minutes. Stir in cumin and cinnamon stick, and toast until aromatic, about 1 minute; add ginger and garlic, and cook until just softened, about 1 minute more.

2 Add carrots, season with salt and freshly ground black pepper, and cook until slightly tender, about 3 minutes. Add tomatoes and their juice, vegetable broth, and saffron and stir to combine. Bring mixture to a simmer and cook, covered, until vegetables are almost completely cooked but still raw in the center, about 7 minutes.

3 Add cauliflower, olives, chickpeas, preserved lemon, and currants and simmer, stirring occasionally, until cauliflower is just tender, about 10 minutes more. Taste tagine and adjust seasoning if necessary.

To serve:

4 Place couscous in a large bowl or baking dish. Bring water to a boil. Once water boils, pour over couscous, and let stand until water is absorbed, about 5 minutes. Add olive oil, season to taste with salt and pepper, and stir briefly to combine.

5 Serve tagine over couscous, topped with almonds and scallions. Pass yogurt on the side.

Servings: 6

Vegetable Tagine

"Mimicking the slow cooking Moroccan tagine, this fast stove top version made with a variety of vegetables and spices, is full of rich flavor and texture. Enjoy this vegetable tagine served on its own as a hearty stew, or with steamed couscous or warm bread"

15 ml	olive oil	3		(16 ounce) cans chicken broth
1	onion, chopped			
1	green bell pepper, chopped	30	ml	lemon juice
		15	ml	honey
3	cloves garlic, chopped	0.5	g	ground cumin
3	carrots, chopped	0.5	g	ground coriander
2	sweet potatoes, chopped	0.6	g	ground turmeric
		0.6	g	ground cinnamon
1	eggplant, chopped	440.2	g	garbanzo beans, rinsed and drained
4	plum tomatoes, chopped			
3	zucchini, chopped	6	g	salt
70 g	raisins	2	g	ground black pepper

Procedure

1 Heat oil in the bottom of a large, heavy pot over medium-high heat . Cook and stir the onion, green bell pepper, and garlic in the oil until tender, about 5 minutes.

2 Place the carrots, sweet potatoes, eggplant, plum tomatoes, zucchini, and raisins in the pot with the onion mixture. Stir in the chicken broth, lemon juice, honey, and season with cumin, coriander, turmeric, and cinnamon. Bring the stew to a boil over high heat, cover, and reduce the heat to medium-low, and simmer until the vegetables are tender, about 30 minutes.

3 Pour the garbanzo beans into the stew and season with salt and pepper. Stir to combine and cook the soup for an additional 10 to 15 minutes.

Servings: 6

Total Time: 75 minutes

Vegetable Tagine With Couscous

1		bundle asparagus, trimmed	2	yellow bell peppers, cored, seeded, and cut into 1
1/2 lb		haricots verts (small French green beans)	1	green bell pepper, cored, seeded, and cut into 1
2	Tbs	olive oil		
1		large yellow onion, peeled, and roughly chopped	5	Japanese eggplants, trimmed, and cut into 1 1/2
5		celery stalks, trimmed, and cut on the diagonal into 1 1/2	7	medium red new potatoes, quartered
2		large carrots, peeled, and thinly sliced, plus	6	oz tomato paste
			1	cup water
4		large carrots, peeled, and cut on the diagonal into 1		Salt, to taste
				Freshly-ground black pepper, to taste
2		large leeks, white and light green part, halved lengthwise, then thinly sliced	4	Tbs minced fresh Italian flat-leaf parsley
			4	Tbs minced fresh basil
12		large mushrooms, quartered	2	boxes couscous - (12 oz ea)
6		garlic cloves, minced or chopped	1/2 cup	hot water, almost simmering, but not boiling
4		ripe tomatoes, diced		

Procedure

1 Bring a pot of water to a boil; add asparagus and cook until just barely tender. Drain and refresh with cold water. Drain again; set aside.

2 Bring pot of water to a boil; add haricots verts and boil until cooked tender-crisp. Drain and refresh with cold water. Drain again; set aside.

3 In a large Dutch oven or pot, add oil. Heat on high heat until very hot, but not smoking. Add onion, celery, 2 thinly sliced carrots, and leeks. Cook on medium-high heat, stirring frequently, until onions are translucent and celery is lightly browned, about 10 minutes.

4 Add mushrooms and garlic; cook 1 minute. Stir in tomatoes, bell peppers, 4 carrots, eggplant and potatoes. Add tomato paste, 1 cup water, salt and pepper. Stir to combine. Bring to boil; lower heat and simmer, covered, until all vegetables are very tender and sauce thickens, about 30 to 40 minutes. Should have a stew-like consistency.

5 Stir in parsley and basil. Taste and adjust seasonings if necessary. Place couscous in a large bowl. Pour 1/2 cup water over top. Add salt and pepper to taste. Toss.

6 Presentation: Place couscous on large serving platter. Top with vegetable tagine mixture. Allow to sit 10 minutes before serving, so that the couscous can absorb some of the liquid. If you have excess juices, serve them in a sauce boat on the side. Garnish with reserved asparagus and haricots verts.

Servings: 12

Vegetable Tagine with Sliced Apricots

1		medium sweet potato -- partially cooked cut into one-inch chunks	8	oz	baby carrots
			1	pinch	cinnamon
			1	pinch	ground ginger
			1/2 tsp		cayenne
1		green bell pepper -- cut into strips	1		lemon -- juice only
			1	tsp	honey
1	lb	tomatoes -- concasser	4		dried apricots -- finely silced
		--x--			**To serve:
1/2	cup	split peas -- yellow, rinsed	1/2 tsp		cumin seed -- toasted
		(or red lentils)			steamed couscous -- such as
1 1/2	cups	vegetable stock			
1		garlic clove -- crushed			
8	oz	pearl onions -- cut to carrot size			

Procedure

1 Cook the potato or yam in microwave, steamer, or oven, as preferred. Let cool. Cut bell pepper into 1-inch rings; core. Then slice rings into strips. Blanch, peel, seed, and chop the tomatoes to measure 2 cups. Peel the potato and cut into 1-inch chunks. In a sauce pan, place the peas or lentils, the stock, garlic and onions; bring to a boil and simmer, covered, for 20 minutes. Stir in all the vegetables, spices, lemon juice, honey, and apricots. Return to a boil, add water if you want more sauce, and simmer for 15 to 20 minutes more. Sprinkle with the toasted cumin seeds and serve in large shallow bowl with room for steamed couscous.

Servings: 4

INDEX*

black peppercorns   107
blanched almonds   25, 57, 78, 91-2
blend   12, 51
boil   13, 22-3, 28, 33-4, 37-8, 41, 50, 71, 77-9, 82, 85-7, 89-
    90, 94-6, 115, 129-30, 136-8 [15]
boil sauce   41
boiler, double   113
boiling   15, 123, 136
  finished meal   17
boiling mixture   13
boiling water   50, 69, 80, 85, 128
boneless chicken thighs   23
boneless lamb shoulder   63, 73, 91-2, 121
boneless lamb stew meat   61, 77
bones   11, 27, 31, 42, 69, 71, 75
book   3-4
bordellos   119
bouillon   48
bowl   23, 25, 50, 58-9, 61, 79-80, 82, 85, 114-15, 128
  heatproof   46
  large   25, 31, 40-1, 65, 108, 133, 137
  small   15, 28, 33, 73
braises   10-11, 61
braising liquid   10
bread, pita   71-2
breast
  diced chicken   103
  skinless boneless chicken   19
  skinless chicken   36
broth   29, 33, 39, 41, 56, 61, 82, 99, 114, 117
browned chicken   23
bubbling   15, 17
bunch   67, 124
butter   14, 28, 33, 42, 62, 67, 71, 78, 80, 82, 91-2, 111, 124,
    126
Buttered Almonds   4, 6, 61-2

C
cabbage   49
café   48
Candied Pumpkin   6, 42-3
Canned chick-peas   71
canned chickpeas   82
  high-quality   132
Canned crushed tomatoes   71

Capers   6, 54
caramelized onion topping   67
Caramelized Sweet Onions   7, 77
carrot size   138
carrots   13, 17, 19, 23, 36-8, 41, 44-5, 49, 51, 56-7, 59-60,
      63, 65-6, 99, 110, 133-4 [9]
  blanch   128
  fresh   51
  large   23, 40, 56, 75, 121, 136
  ounces   113
  shredded   84
cashews   46
casserole   19, 34, 75, 101, 117
  heatproof   101
  vegetable   52
cauliflower   15, 19, 128, 132-3
Cauliflower Tagine   6, 15-16
cayenne   27-8, 56, 59
cayenne pepper   59, 99, 110, 113
  dash   99
celery   19, 57, 137
chermoula paste   101
chick-peas   71
Chick Peas   7, 123
chicken   6-8, 11, 17, 19, 21-3, 25-9, 31-4, 37-45, 49-50, 80,
      82, 84-8, 99, 103-6, 108-9, 112 [4]
chicken bouillon cube   19
chicken breasts   17, 38
  brown   27
  large boneless skinless   80
chicken broth   22-3, 45, 60, 105, 134
  canned   94, 96
  cans   134
  cups low-salt   40
  cups lowfat   33
  homemade   59
  low-sodium   44
  low-sodium fat-free   117
  ml   23
  reduced-sodium   29
chicken cooks   26, 28
chicken cubes   129
  baked   129
chicken filet   129
chicken mixture   80, 112

chicken/spice mixture   37
chicken stock   13, 37, 63, 79, 85-6, 89, 104
   free   36
   ml   80
chicken stock- Marigold Swiss Vegetable Bouillon   103
chicken stock sticks cinnamon, hot   46
Chicken Tagine   6, 17-41
chicken thighs   29-30, 49
   bone-in   29
   boneless skinless   105
   broiler-fryer   112
   skinless boneless   40
chickpeas   6-7, 12-14, 57, 63, 65-6, 82, 126-7, 132-3
   chopped   13
   cooked   65, 126, 132
   dry   13
chile pepper, green   29
chiles, green   22
chilli   104
chopped cilantro   27-8, 36, 56, 65
chopped coriander   57, 78-80, 114, 127
chopped fresh cilantro   13, 29, 31, 44, 94, 96, 105-6, 115
chopped green onions   13
chopped onions   13, 36, 49, 57, 77, 87, 119
chopped parsley   52, 58, 61, 82
chunks   55, 65, 82, 99, 101-3, 117, 119
cilantro   13, 30-1, 34, 37, 45, 51-2, 61, 65, 67-8, 86, 95-6,
      106, 110, 115
cilantro sprigs   27-8
cinnamon   6, 23, 29, 34, 38, 42, 44-5, 49, 54, 56, 59, 61, 66-
      7, 69, 76, 112-13 [6]
Cinnamon Gourmet   7, 73-4
cinnamon sticks   25-8, 38, 46, 56, 58, 61, 65-6, 71, 73, 77,
      79, 82, 87, 91-2, 112-13, 132-3 [2]
citrons confits   48
clay cooking pot   17
Clay pots   116
clay tagine   17
cloves   22, 59, 61, 107
   large garlic   40
   medium garlic   51-2
cloves garlic   13, 17, 21, 29, 34, 36, 57-9, 63, 85, 99, 112-
      13, 117, 126, 128, 134
Coarsely-chopped onion   42
coat   25, 28, 31, 51, 59, 66, 115

fork   23, 46, 51, 66-7, 80, 106, 112
fresh cilantro   25, 34, 51-2, 67
fresh coriander   98, 113, 124, 130
fresh ginger   33, 51, 128
   grated   44, 132
fresh lemon juice   31, 51, 82, 89, 107
frozen barbecued chickens   84
frozen chopped peppers   84
fry   21, 49, 55, 58, 79, 87, 102, 104, 124-5, 130
frying   103-4, 130

G
garbanzo beans   13, 99, 105-6, 134
garlic
   clove   67
   crushed   115
   fresh   60
   medium cloves   132
   minced   56, 89, 108, 112, 128, 131
   teaspoon   131
garlic cloves   14-15, 19, 25, 27, 31, 38, 44, 65, 79, 91-2, 94,
      96, 101, 103, 128, 130 [2]
garlic powder   59, 84
garlic salt   23
garnish   17, 22, 27, 31-4, 44-5, 56, 66, 68, 84, 89-90, 105-6,
      115, 137
ginger   11, 14, 21, 23, 25, 28-9, 33-4, 42, 44-5, 49, 51, 56,
      58-60, 62, 76-7, 91-2 [13]
golden   26, 41, 52, 58, 64, 67, 70, 73, 79, 94, 126, 129
golden raisins   6, 67-8, 102, 105
grated ginger   14, 59
greased tagine   78
green olives   6, 29-30, 36, 119, 132
   cracked   61, 89
ground   13, 23, 38, 44, 57, 61, 77-8, 85, 102, 121, 133-4
ground cayenne pepper   110
ground cinnamon   11-12, 25, 46, 59, 77, 87, 91-2, 102, 110,
      134
   good-quality   67
ground coriander   12, 59, 79, 99, 102, 134
ground cumin   23, 59, 63, 94, 102, 108, 110, 115, 134
   teaspoons   40, 106
   tsp 7.5ml   105
ground ginger   23, 46, 59, 102, 108, 110
   teaspoons   40

tsp 1.3ml   42, 94
ground pepper   15, 29, 31, 34, 67, 71, 131
ground turmeric   59, 110, 134

H
halved crosswise   121
halves
  boneless chicken breast   99
  skinless chicken breast   22
haricots verts   136-7
harissa   6, 65-6, 80, 127
heat   13-15, 23, 26-7, 29, 33-4, 40-1, 49-50, 66-7, 69-71,
    86-7, 89-90, 94-6, 108, 115-17, 124-6, 131 [22]
  distribute   116
  high   10, 34, 52, 61, 69, 77, 91-2, 94, 96, 106, 117, 121,
    124-5, 134, 137
  low   15, 17, 38, 42, 67, 77, 82, 98, 102, 108, 119, 123,
    129
  lower   137
  medium-low   63, 98, 121
  moderately-high   19, 75
  turn   71
heat butter   25
heat cumin   54
heat-diffuser   116
Heat oil   14, 22, 28, 38, 63, 66, 77, 94, 96, 134
heat olive oil   23, 132
heat oven   101, 131
heated oil   23
Herbed Couscous   29
hob   46, 50, 101
homes   120-1
honey   7, 11, 25-6, 42, 56, 58, 60, 65, 69-70, 73, 76, 78-9,
    84, 87-8, 91-3, 101 [3]
hot chile peppers, red   51
Hot red pepper   123
hours   13-14, 23, 31, 34, 39, 42, 45-6, 55-61, 63, 66-7, 71,
    77-9, 91-2, 102, 104, 112-13 [5]
huile   48

I
ice-water bath   108
ingredients   4, 10-12, 38, 40, 49, 57, 66-7, 85, 106, 128-30

J

jar   83, 107, 132
juices   12-13, 21-2, 26, 28, 33, 40, 47, 56-7, 63, 70, 80, 99,
    108, 112, 129, 132-3 [1]

K
kitchen strings   25, 67

L
lamb   6-7, 11, 55-63, 66-8, 71, 73, 75, 77-9, 89-92, 94, 97,
    102, 113, 119, 121, 124 [1]
  brown   56, 63
  coat   71
  diced   57, 59
  ground   98
  lean   55
  return   61, 63, 76
Lamb & Pear Tagine   6, 55
Lamb and Prune Tagine Recipe   6, 57
lamb bones   75
lamb cutlets   78
lamb meat   59, 102
lamb sausage   44
Lamb Shallot   6, 58
lamb shanks   11
  gm   71
lamb shoulder   65, 89, 124
  bone-in   61
lamb shoulder chops   75
lamb stew meat   67, 69
lamb stock   58, 79
  ml   58
Lamb Tagine   4, 6-7, 59-77, 124
Lamb Tajine   7, 78
Large chicken thighs   49
lavash   71-2
lean lamb leg steak   113
leeks   101, 103-4, 137
Leg of lamb   58
legs   27, 31, 55, 67, 79
Lemon & Olives   6, 31-2
lemon rind   58, 63, 79
lemon slices   19, 33
lemon water   40
lemon wedges   12, 27, 80
lemon zest   33, 60, 80

pearl onions   69
  frozen   128
pears   11, 55, 102, 124
peel   31, 34, 42, 69, 115, 138
peel chick peas   123
pepper   13-15, 17, 19, 22, 29-31, 40-1, 44, 54, 63, 66-8, 70-
    1, 75-8, 80, 86-7, 89, 130-1 [19]
  green   22, 121
  teaspoon   67, 73
  white   36, 57, 82, 105-6
pepper softens   15
pepper.Cook   14
petits pois   48
piment doux   48
pinch ground ginger   138
Pinch of ground cumin   115
pinch saffron   57, 79
pinch saffron threads   33, 65, 73, 75, 121, 132
pinch salt   51, 57
Pine Nut   28, 44-5, 63, 80, 89-90
pink   19, 94, 96, 106
pint   46, 50
pint lamb stock   79
pitted Green peppers   119
pitted prunes   14, 56, 69, 71, 75, 110, 124
Place carrots   37
Place chicken   22
Place couscous   133, 137
Place pot   61
plate   12, 19, 25-8, 31, 44, 47, 59, 63, 68, 75, 86, 95-6
platter   28, 68-9, 120, 137
plum tomatoes   134
  chopped   77
poach iti   124-5
poivre   48
pork   94, 96
pork mixture   95-6
pot   21, 41, 45, 56, 60-2, 69-70, 73, 75, 82, 86-7, 91-2, 102,
    119, 121, 126, 134 [1]
  heavy   28, 73, 91-2, 134
pot of water   136
potato   138
potatoes   17, 21, 29, 56, 65-6, 98, 115, 118-19, 126, 136-7
  sweet   117, 134
potent cheese taste   111

Rewarm tagine   41
rice   13, 21, 38, 55, 66, 70, 102, 112, 126-7
rinse   13, 34, 38, 51, 128
Roast Peppers   6, 36-7
Roma tomatoes   21
root vegetables   11

S
saffron   11-12, 14, 28, 33-4, 42, 49, 52, 56, 58-9, 61, 65, 69,
     71, 77-9, 91-2, 126 [11]
   pinch ground   89
   powdered   78, 94, 96, 124
   tsp 1.3ml Ground   42
saffron threads   27, 36, 108
   crumbled   77, 91-2, 105-6
saffron threads juice   85
safran   48
salt
   chopped   125
   coarse   85, 107-8, 111, 131
   kosher   59, 61, 82
   sliced   31
   sprinkle   107
   tablespoon   107
   teaspoons   25, 92
   tsp 2.5ml   105
salt-and-lemon-juice mixture   132
sauce   10, 28, 41-2, 48, 51, 63, 70, 73, 78, 82, 84, 86-8, 98,
     124-5, 138
sauce ingredients   98
saucepan   23, 33, 42, 69, 111, 128
   large   33, 55, 108, 113
sausage   44-5
saute   36, 38, 86-7
saute chicken   38
Saute onion   21, 36
sauté   13, 17, 40-1, 44, 77, 131
sea salt   82
   coarse   107
season   15, 17, 29-30, 34, 41, 66-8, 71, 73, 76-8, 86, 89, 99,
     102, 108, 128-31, 133-4 [4]
season chicken   22
season vegetables   121
seasonings   11, 14, 45, 72, 115, 133, 137
seeds

Spicy Potato Tagine 7, 115-16
spoon 47, 53, 68, 83, 86, 111, 113
sprigs 25, 68, 98
Spring Vegetables 6-7, 40-1, 128
sprinkle 17, 27-8, 41-2, 44, 46, 51, 54, 64, 66, 70-1, 78, 84, 95-6, 101, 106, 111-12 [3]
sprinkle chicken 40
squash 42, 71, 76, 86, 98-9
 butternut 42, 99
 yellow 75, 85, 131
steamed couscous 134, 138
 toasted 138
stew 12-13, 36, 57, 64, 68, 70, 76-7, 91-2, 102, 107, 134
stick 37, 91-2, 112
stir 13-15, 23, 28, 30-1, 37-8, 44-5, 49-50, 60, 66, 68-70, 72-3, 79-80, 89-92, 95-6, 133-4, 137-8 [13]
stirring 15, 19, 25-6, 28-9, 31, 34, 54, 63, 73, 75-7, 91-2, 94, 96, 124-5, 131, 133 [13]
stock 13, 37-9, 46, 66, 80, 86, 89, 103-4, 138
stovetop 10, 36
strain 34, 70, 82, 111
String 124-5
strips 19, 31, 46, 105, 121, 138
 green pepper 121
 thin 22, 59
sucre 48
sugar 52, 67, 71, 99, 131
sun-dried tomatoes 15
 chopped 106
 chopped drained 105
 sliced oil-packed 15
supermarkets 127-8
sweet onions 67
 chopped 77
sweet potato 75
Sweet Potato Tagine 7, 117-18

T
tablespoon butter 80
tablespoon ground coriander 40
tablespoon juice 37
tablespoon oil 25, 27-9, 75
tablespoons 19, 21, 25, 27, 40-1, 49, 54, 57, 59, 75, 77, 80, 89, 106, 113, 115
tablespoons golden raisins 106

Breinigsville, PA USA
07 February 2010
232079BV00003B/86/P

9 781921 573583